## About the Author

Born and raised on council estates, Mike Greene has worked hard to achieve his success within the business world. As well as being an accomplished and well-known business entrepreneur and angel investor, Mike is also a Director/Chairman of nine companies, including Dot.com, trade associations, charities, marketing and retail organisations. He is a global retail/shopper consultant, an international speaker, a professional mentor, a philanthropist, an endurance adventurer, a passionate charity fundraiser and a dedicated family man with his wife Julia and their two daughters.

In 2011/12 Mike starred as one of Channel 4's Secret Millionaires. Following the programme, which had a great impact on him, he sold his main business and took a three month sabbatical with the personal challenge to raise £100,000 for 100 charities in 100 days. He was successful in this bid and was inspired to go on to commit one-third of his time to helping charities and mentoring people to change their lives for the better. Mike Greene's ambition is to help others achieve their goals by sharing his stories and experiences through inspirational public speaking and personal and professional mentoring.

Jo

Life is a journey

Enjoy it!

Mike.

Start your Transition now

**www.mikegreene.co.uk**

# MIKE GREENE

## FAILURE BREEDS
## SUCCESS

PG Press  - PGP

Published by PG Press (PGP)
Mountain Farmhouse, Marden Road,
Marden, Kent TN12 9PZ
Telephone: +44 (0) 1622 831310
info@professionalghost.co.uk
www.professionalghost.org

© Mike Greene 2013

Printed by
Berforts Group - Stevenage and Hastings

ISBN – 978-0-9575476-1-2

To Julia. My wife, my best friend and my motivation

## Acknowledgements

It's hard to recognise any one individual when in reality we are all a sum total of all the experiences we have had to date. However, I can list a few people without which my success and this book would never have happened:

- My Mum, who was told to put me and my brother/sisters into care after my dad left, because they didn't think that she could bring so many young children up alone. They clearly didn't know what a strong, inspirational and dedicated woman she was. She has always, and continues to believe in me, inspire me, and love me. She taught me tough love but with unlimited affection.

- Les Hooper, the newsagent that gave me a chance and, through his belief in me, gave me belief in myself.

- Ray and Nicky Chamberlain. Their friendship never had a price, but was priceless, and when Julia and I had nothing, they gave us shelter and a job. The Maslovian foundation that enabled us to start again, without which we may never have built the life we enjoy today

- My wife Julia. Without her unfaltering patience, support and love over the last twenty years of marriage, it wouldn't have happened and wouldn't be worth it.

- Teena Lyons at Professional Ghost for being able to turn my passionate but jumbled beliefs and ramblings into a book that will hopefully help many others achieve their goals and dreams.

Finally, let's not forget all the critics, cynics, skeptics and pessimists. It is their barriers and bleating that drove me to achieve. These naysayers are the balance to all the positive in the world, the night that balances day, the famine that helps us appreciate the feast. My sincere thanks to them for, without them, I may have accepted a life of mediocrity and dependency.

# CONTENTS

# INTRODUCTION

The timing could not have been worse. I was just hours away from giving a speech to 2000 travel agents in Portugal and I had still not written a word of what I would say. I had decided to work from home so I could give my talk my full, albeit last-minute, attention. Then, in a scenario all occasional home workers will recognise, disaster struck. My eldest daughter, Rosie, fell ill and couldn't go to school. With my wife away, I was the only childcare option immediately available.

Weighing up the empty sheet of paper in front of me and the barrage of demands from Rosie, I had the desperate feeling of a doomed man. My company had been keen to get into the travel business for years and I was at the threshold of a fantastic opportunity to get some attention among the opinion formers who counted. Yet, I didn't have a clue what to say and now I didn't have any time to think about it either.

In desperation I cast around for something with which to distract Rosie for a few much-needed hours. Grabbing one of the hitherto unopened travel magazines in front of me, I flicked through it for inspiration. Spotting a colourful map of the world, I tore out the page and then ripped it into dozens of tiny pieces.

'There you are, darling,' I said, presenting the pile of shredded paper to my rather perplexed-looking daughter. 'It's a map of the world. See if you can put it together, like a jigsaw, and I will play with you once you have finished.'

Rosie nodded and disappeared into a corner while I, with a sigh of relief, turned to my empty page.

fbs@mikegreene.co.uk

Less than ten minutes later, Rosie returned to my office carrying a neatly sellotaped map of the world.

'What?' I exclaimed. I was utterly mystified by how she had done this so quickly. I had thought she'd be occupied for hours. 'How did you do that so fast?'

'I looked at the back of the page and there was a picture of people on it,' she said, smiling.

Then, with childish simplicity, she added: 'Once I got the people right, the world came right too.'

Suddenly, I had one of those eureka moments. One of those 'that's it!' flashes of inspiration. My nine-year-old had articulated something that had been at the back of my mind for years: *if you get rid of all the distractions, fears and noise and make the person right, the world and everything around you will come right, too.*

In other words, if you sort yourself out first, everything will fall into place.

When things go wrong, it is very easy to blame this or that environmental factor, or a lack of opportunity, or a failure in your upbringing, or any one of a hundred different culprits. It's easy to say, 'I can't put this right because…' or 'I failed because….' We rarely examine ourselves closely to gauge our own roles in the world.

The reason I was thinking in this way was that I have long been fascinated by failure.

It seems that everyone fears failure. To most people it is the worst thing in the world that can happen. Indeed, the majority of us don't like to even mention our failures. For some, the feeling of embarrassment and shame when things don't go to plan can be too much to bear and can drag them to the depths of despair.

I have long harboured the notion that failure is not a bad thing. In fact, it is actually a very important part of our life journey. Failure teaches you some of the most important lessons you will ever learn, and if you are only attuned to these lessons you will emerge a stronger, wiser and more resilient person. In fact, you will be equipped with all the ingredients for success.

The reason for my fascination with the notion of failure, and people's fear of it, is in large part down to my own experiences. Most people know me as a highly successful businessman with a career running a multi-million-pound retail consultancy, plus more than half a dozen directorships and numerous business-angel investments under my belt, but my own personal story runs much deeper than this. I was by no means born with a silver spoon in my mouth and have had to work hard every step of the way to achieve what I have done.

Along the way, I have seen some spectacular failures.

It was my appearance in Channel 4's *Secret Millionaire* programme in October 2011 that really consolidated my thinking about my past and its effect on what I have subsequently achieved. In the programme, I returned to Peterborough, the city where I was brought up, and got involved with various groups that were trying to help underprivileged youngsters. It was a deeply moving experience on many levels and I was very affected by how selfless some people can be in giving so much of their time and emotions to these causes. The volunteers really were inspirational.

Yet, it was the kids themselves that were the real eye-opener. Most of them had had a really tough start to their lives and all of them had some real challenges to contend with. However, the ways they chose to deal with these challenges were very different. For some kids, the scars of what had gone before were too deeply ingrained for them to move on; however, others I met through *Secret Millionaire* were clearly made stronger by the experience. When given half a chance, they showed that they still had the mental and physical strength not to give up and that they wouldn't let everything that had gone on in the past drag them down. They proved this by grabbing any opportunity presented to them with both hands and moving on with joy and enthusiasm. It was a rare quality indeed, but some of the kids I met on the show refused to be defined by what had gone before. Watching these characters blossom when given a helping hand was an immensely emotionally affecting experience.

Seeing just how far it is possible to turn things around – from an apparently hopeless situation into a new, prosperous beginning – raised some interesting parallels with my own formative years. Like I said, I wasn't born into a life of wealth and privilege. Indeed, my father abandoned the family home when I was just a few years old, which led to my mother and us kids being evicted and then housed for months in an old people's care home until we could be rehoused in cramped, rented accommodation. In fact, it wasn't until the family moved to Peterborough, when I was 11 years old, that I finally got a bed to myself and no longer had to share with my siblings.

Despite these tough early years, I always swore that I would be a successful businessman when I grew up. Even as a young boy, I told my mother that one day I would be a millionaire. And I really believed it, too.

As I grew older, I worked hard, doing every job I could lay my hands on: washing cars, picking potatoes, paper rounds, milk rounds, collecting scrap metals to sell and so on. Gradually, I did manage to establish myself in business and even scraped together some money to buy a couple of properties to rent out. By my early twenties, anyone looking in from the outside world would have said I was showing clear promise of better things to come. Then, catastrophe struck. Despite successfully growing a franchise business, I learned the very harsh lesson that a business is more likely to fail from lack of cash than lack of sales. In trying to grow my business too quickly, I made the mistake of starving it of cash and found that what I had left couldn't support the growth. After months of trying to make it work, with my wife Julia and I juggling minimal cash and seemingly endless payments, we finally had to close the doors on the business.

I was devastated, but my one consolation was that I still had a house that had been let to tenants. At least, I thought, this would provide a home and basis to start again. Alas, to my horror, when I returned to inspect the property, I discovered that the tenants had abandoned it following a fire in the kitchen. No one had seen fit to mention to me that the ground floor of my property had been virtually destroyed.

It was a massive blow, but I still hung on to the belief that it would be OK in the end, because the house was insured. However, when I spoke to the insurer, it emerged that I had made the gravest of errors. I had mistakenly insured my rental property as a private dwelling, and as soon as I told the company that my tenants had caused the fire, the case was effectively closed. I was left with a massive bill, a mortgage I couldn't afford and a property I couldn't rent.

After that, my life seemed to spiral out of control. In my desperation I made a couple of other daft business decisions and, before I knew it, I hit rock bottom. Aged just 27, I was declared bankrupt. My young wife Julia and I were forced to rely on the charity of friends, and after a period of weeks living back at home with my mother we moved into rented accommodation and delivered pizzas just to survive.

Looking back at this period, I can still vividly remember how wretched and lost I felt for a brief time. When it first happened, I believed I had sunk so low that I would probably never recover. But I did. Even now, I am not sure what the first spark was, but one day I suddenly realised that I didn't have to define myself by my failure. I wasn't 'Mike Greene the bankrupt', I was 'Mike Greene the entrepreneur', with huge potential and a dream of being a millionaire. Unless I got out from under my failure, I would never even get close to that aspiration.

And that is exactly what I did. However, I didn't achieve what I went on to achieve by forgetting what I had learned in those early years. Just as the saying goes, what doesn't kill you makes you stronger, and I resolved to use what I had experienced to help pull myself out of the mire and succeed against all the odds.

In the ensuing years I worked my way up the corporate ladder, primarily in the retail industry, a journey that culminated in growing him!, an international retail consultancy that advises global and leading UK retailers, suppliers and manufacturers on people's shopping habits. The business went from strength to strength, expanding into USA, Australia and New Zealand before being sold to publishing giant William Reed in 2011.

Since then, I have gone plural, as the expression goes, and now have nine directorships and divide much of the rest of my time between mentoring other business people and charity work.

This experience, coupled with that on *Secret Millionaire,* inspired me to write this book. In *Failure Breeds Success,* I set out to use lessons I learned from my early experiences (through to building him!) together with *Secret Millionaire* to look more deeply into the notion of failure. I hope to show that even the most catastrophic of situations can actually turn out to be the best thing that can ever happen.

It is my contention that no one should allow themselves to be written off, however bad life seems, because we all have the ability to turn any setback into triumph.

*Failure Breeds Success* is a self-help book, aimed at a broad audience. Although it has many lessons that will resonate with business people and entrepreneurs, it will also be a valuable and motivating pick-me-up for anyone who is struggling to find direction in life, or who feels they have been written off. The processes presented here should encourage you to set out the goals you most want to achieve in life – however ambitious they might be – and then attain them using the sum total of your life experiences in a positive way.

Step by step, this book shows you how to deal with what has happened in your past and how to plan for your ideal future without being hampered by fear of failure. There are ideas on setting out quantifiable goals, averting the naysayers and changing the way you view your day-to-day efforts forever. By getting away from things and looking at them afresh, you can find a totally new perspective on your life.

One of the difficulties of embarking on a project like this is that we are all so different. Although I am trained in behavioural profiling (and indeed the science of behaviour was the backbone of my him! business), I, like you, don't need a complex formula to know that we all react to events differently. When things turn sour, everyone seems to have their own way of dealing with the situation, both outwardly and inwardly. Some people will react with quiet stoicism, while others will border on hysteria. Others will respond in a different fashion entirely.

The same goes for any sort of planning for the future. Everyone has a different stance on setting and achieving their goals.

However, if you take away the raw emotion, there are common threads to how we could and should plan our lives and deal with failure and mistakes along the way. It is my belief that, if you understand a bit more about the type of person you are and how you react to outside stimuli, you will be able to learn how to get the most out of the best and worst things that happen to you. It is for this reason that this book has been written in conjunction with the leading behavioural science group Thomas International.

One of the Thomas International instruments that I have found particularly useful is the Personal Profile Analysis (PPA). This is not a test but a work-based questionnaire that provides an indication of your preferred behavioural style when tackling a task. The information produced has been invaluable to me, not only in developing my self-awareness but also in understanding others who may have a very different approach to my own. Building strong and effective relationships – whether with your bank manager, customers, suppliers, staff or peers – is a vital ingredient of success. And anyone who takes their work style home with them may find the information useful in the family situation too!

There are four main PPA groups – dominant, influencer, steadiness and compliance – and I will give you a brief outline of them in a moment. When you go through them you may recognise yourself from their descriptions, although most of us are a bit of a mix. However, we do tend to be stronger in one group than the others and to be defined by one group to a significant degree. If you would like to get the full picture as it relates to you, you can complete a PPA by visiting my website: www.mikegreene.co.uk/ppa. However, a rough outline of the groups follows.

*Dominant* people focus on achieving results and are likely to be assertive, competitive, direct, driving, forceful and inquisitive self-starters. Above all, they strive to avoid failure, so on occasion they may be aggressive and overbearing, and may be ready and willing to make gut decisions without necessarily considering the effect(s) of those decisions on other people. They are motivated by power and control, so this book should suit them because it gives them total responsibility for delivering the success they crave.

*Influencers* are people who focus on relationships. They tend to be verbally communicative, friendly, persuasive, positive and optimistic networkers who will approach you rather than wait for you to approach them. Because they strive to avoid rejection, they may sometimes find it hard to make tough or unpopular decisions. They are motivated by public recognition and this book is likely to appeal to them because it emphasises the importance of building relationships with high-profile mentors in pursuit of one's dreams.

*Steadiness* people focus on consistent support or service delivery, often of a specialist nature, and tend to be dependable, deliberate, methodical, thorough, persistent, patient and kind. They really listen and like to finish whatever they have started. Because they strive to avoid insecurity, they can sometimes seem resistant to change. They are motivated by security, so the step-by-step structure of this book should reassure them that following the process will lead to the desired goal.

*Compliance* people focus on quality and standards, often of a technical nature. They tend to be careful, systematic, precise, accurate and logical perfectionists. Because they strive to avoid direct conflict and confrontation, they can sometimes seem quite rigid and rule-bound. They are motivated by standard operating procedures, preferably written. Therefore, this book's detailed transition map, showing the planned stages from present to future states, should inspire their confidence.If you want to get into what this book could offer you in more detail, there is a section at the end of each chapter that will help you to customise the content to your own particular personality type. The advice here in *Failure Breeds Success* will work in isolation, without the behavioural science part, but to get the maximum benefit you may like to use it with the end-of-chapter advice written for your specific group, so that the book is entirely tailored to your needs.

Overall, I firmly believe that, if you commit to a little hard work and application, *Failure Breeds Success* will change everything you have ever thought about failing and will free you to meet and exceed your personal goals, however ambitious they may be. Instead of dismissing failure as a stigma, or something that has to be avoided at all costs, we should all be welcoming it as a stepping stone to success and gratification.

To triumph in the modern world, we all need to fail. Not just once, but again and again. The trick is training yourself to reframe your thinking, recognise any foul-ups and use your experiences to come out even stronger.

There is no success without failure. It's time to embrace your failings and reach your goals. This book will show you how.

**CHAPTER ONE**

# FIRST DEFINE SUCCESS

Rediscover your life with fresh eyes.

**Suc-cess**

Noun:    1. The accomplishment of an aim or purpose

2. The attainment of popularity or profit[1]

My brother Leroy has been travelling from pretty much the moment he reached adulthood. He'll be in the UK for a couple of months, grafting on building sites or working in shops or as a deliveryman – anything, in fact, just to build up a few thousand pounds. Then, once he thinks he has enough cash in his pocket, he'll say his goodbyes and be off to some exotic location like India or Cambodia, where he will stay for months at a time.

A couple of years ago, when he was briefly back in the UK, I took him to one side to ask him a question that had been on my mind for a while.

---

1 Dictionary.com.

We had just had a pleasant and convivial family meal and I figured that now was as good a time as any for a brotherly chat.

'Listen, mate, when are you going settle down and take life seriously,' I began, putting a friendly hand onto Leroy's shoulder. 'You're nearly forty now and really need to start laying down some roots.'

He spun around and looked at me as though I had suddenly grown another head.

'What makes you think I want your life?' he asked, with genuine surprise, his eyes wide and with just the trace of a smile at the corners of his mouth. 'I have never, ever, done anything I don't want to do. I love my life and would be perfectly content with what I have done if I died tomorrow.'

For a moment, I was utterly taken aback. I hadn't expected this answer at all. But the shock of Leroy's response forced me to think more deeply about what he had just said.

For as far back as I can remember, I have had very clear and defined ideas about success. I can recall telling my mum very firmly, when I was just seven or eight years old, that I was going to be a millionaire one day. All credit to my mum, she didn't discourage me from my ideal, even though in those days we barely had enough money to put food on the table. Over the years, through hard work, guts and determination (notwithstanding a few hiccups along the way), I did achieve this goal. I have made my millions, and to an outsider looking in I have all the trappings of success. I have a large house in the country and several homes abroad, I have nice cars and I take fancy holidays. I have achieved all I set out to do and more.

The big question is, though, am I more *successful* than my brother?

The truth, when it dawned on me, hit me like a lightning bolt. Although I had never considered it until that moment, my brother is actually one of the most successful people I have ever met. He is doing exactly what he wants to do and is exactly where he wants to be. What is more, he is doing it without hurting other people or being dependent on any handouts. He is fulfilling his ambitions and loving every minute of it.

How many people do you know who can say all of that? Indeed, can *you* say that?

It occurred to me then that, before we can make harsh judgements about whether we are a failure or have achieved our goals, we need to have our own individual definition of success. Your own definition of success will be different from mine, just as mine is 180 degrees away from Leroy's. That's just fine. If you have always wanted to be a nurse and have become one, or have always aimed to run your own business and now do so, then you are a success.

The most important thing is to recognise what success looks like for you.

Think about it like this. If you want to turn your perceived failures into success, you need to understand what success means for you. After all, there is little point in setting out on any journey unless you have a clear idea of your destination. If you don't know where you are going, you will end up becoming lost, demoralised and frustrated. Unless you have a clear vision of success, you cannot work towards it.

Other people cannot define success for you – as I discovered when I unwittingly tried to shoehorn my brother into my way of life. Success is achieving what you want to do in the way you want to do it.

Starting to think differently about success is the first step to changing your views on failure.

## Getting started

The trap most people fall into when you ask them to define success is to talk about it in monetary terms. Their automatic reply to questions about how they will know they've made it is 'when I've got a million pounds in the bank' or 'when I have a mansion in the country' or 'when I buy my first Ferrari'.

If you think about it more deeply, though, these are just definitions of what the money you earn will *give* you. Money is only an indicator of success, after all. You can do great work without being paid a penny and may even derive more pleasure from it than you do from your super-successful day job.

Defining success in monetary terms actually shows that what really matters to you is security, or safety, or demonstrating to your peers that you have made it.

Likewise, some people may shoot back that their vision of success is 'doing what I love'. Well, that might be true, but think about this definition more profoundly for a moment. Let's say your hobby is playing the drums. If you did that full time, no doubt you'd feel very happy, wouldn't you? But would that fulfil your other life goals, such as feeding your family and providing them with shelter, clothing and a decent standard of living?

You'd get the same narrow view of success if you simply defined it from the viewpoint of doing well at your career. While I have always loved my job and have put in some pretty hefty hours in my time, if that was my only definition of success, I would have ended up a complete workaholic. I would have missed out on valuable time with my family, which, as it happens, is just as important to me.

No, to get a more accurate view of what success means to each of us, we must dig a bit deeper and look at all of our values in life. We need to understand all the things that are important to us.

To help you define your own measures of success, I have devised the questionnaire below. Set aside some time to fill it in, take your time and answer honestly. Don't be tempted to skip this part because you think you know exactly how you'd define success and don't need it. I guarantee that if you set aside some time to do it – and do it properly – you will discover things about yourself that you haven't previously recognised. Plus, if you skip this stage, although you will find the rest of this book interesting, it will probably be of little real value to you. Missing out the questionnaire will lay a shaky foundation for the future success we will build through this book.

Also, don't succumb to the urge to bring in a relative, or your life partner, so you can answer the questions together. Although two heads are undoubtedly better than one in some cases, this is something that you need to tackle alone. You need to answer these questions from a position where you are not held back, or hamstrung, by the need to be seen to be going one way or another, or by trying to please others. This is about you.

If you still need any encouragement to get started, here is one final thought. How much time did you spend planning and preparing for your holiday this year? I'd imagine it was a good few hours once you'd surfed the net for a while, browsed some brochures and magazines and chatted about it with the family. So, don't you think it is worth spending at least the same amount of time planning what you are going to do with the rest of your life? Or are you prepared to accept that holidays will always be better than 'real' life?

So, let's get started.

### Questionnaire: defining success
1.  If you knew with 100 per cent cast-iron certainty that you couldn't fail, what would you attempt? (list five things)
2.  If money was no object, how would you live your life differently? (list five things)
3.  If you had a million pounds and everything you felt you needed in life, would you still be doing the job you are doing now? If no, what you would be doing?
4.  Which of your relationships is most important to you? Your relationship with your family, your peers or your boss?
5.  What are the most important things in your life right now? (list five things)
6.  List five things or places that you most often daydream about.

7.  If you were at the end of your life and had achieved your wildest dreams, which achievements would you be most proud of?
8.  List five characteristics of the people that you most admire and that you would like to emulate.
9.  If you had unlimited time, what would you spend your time doing? (list five things)
10. List five things that would make the perfect day.
11. Where in the world would you live if you had no ties to your current home?
12. If, 100 years after you died, you were remembered for just one thing, what would it be?

When you look through your answers, a common thread should emerge regarding all the things that you value most in life. To focus your mind further, you may like to list your five answers that resonate with you the most. If you have answered accurately and honestly, it should be obvious what you have to aim for.

Next try to sum up your definition of success in a sentence. It could be something like:

*Make enough money to provide for my family while doing something that allows me to sleep at night.*

*or*

*Make a living and a difference doing what I love.*

*or*

*Doing what I love and making good money at it, while achieving a balance in my life between work, family, health and spirituality.*

There are loads of possible definitions of success. Some people may value financial success more than success in other areas. Others may be more focused on social success, or health success, or spiritual success. It doesn't matter which area or areas your desires fall into. The important thing is that you have made a start and know how you define your own success.

One of the secrets to success is mindset. You will find that deciding where you are going to go and what you need to do makes a huge difference. You will start feeling successful immediately.

Although it is important to give due time and consideration to this process, don't tie yourself into knots in the belief that it has to be 100 per cent right first time. It is possible, indeed quite likely, that your definition of suc-

## QUICK EXERCISE

### If you want to get there fast, take a taxi!

When you climb into a taxi, the first thing you tell the driver is where you want to go. Otherwise, you'd simply be sitting there and wasting everyone's time. You'd be paying waiting time too, because doing nothing doesn't come for free. Yet, when you say to the driver 'take me to the station', the driver doesn't analyse whether or not that is a good destination. He, or she, just gets on with it, delivering you to the station in the shortest possible time.

Imagine, then, that your subconscious is your very own taxi driver. He is sitting there, waiting patiently to know where to take you. The subconscious mind doesn't know right from wrong. It won't judge or offer an alternative. It is literal. You can tell it where to take you, just as you would tell a taxi driver to take you to the station. Therefore, if you tell your creative subconscious that you want something, it will work out the quickest route there. If you have a burning desire to do something, you will achieve it.

Look at it another way. Say money is a bit tight right now. Every time you even think about money, you get a knot in the pit of your stomach. But the problem is that the 'for hire' light in your subconscious is always on. Your subconscious is always listening and it will follow the direction of your negative thoughts – even if you don't intend it to – just as though you were directing your taxi to its destination. So, what are you telling your subconscious mind to do? You are telling it to keep money tight for you and, funnily enough, it will be. If your subconscious closes down all options that would involve money, it will prevent the conscious mind from finding a solution.

This is why it is so important to visualise your goals and make a plan. If you want to get somewhere quickly, it is always best to take a taxi!

cess will change as you go through this process and beyond. That's not a problem, because at least you will be heading in the right direction. Plus, you will now have momentum.

Momentum is very important in this process because, as you will see, things get easier as you go along. Think of it like this: If you were trying to push a broken-down car, it would be virtually impossible to start it moving if the steering wheel were locked. Regardless of whether you ultimately intended to go to the right or to the left, you would have to start by going straight. However, you would discover that, once you were moving, it would be much easier to turn in another direction.

So, it really doesn't matter if your definition of success is not entirely right just now, or does not reflect where you will ultimately want to end up. The important thing is that you have got started. If you were to wait until you were absolutely certain of the direction in which you wanted to go, and then tried to head that way, you would never have been able to get out of first gear.

### Starting the transition to the successful you

Now we have some idea of what we want out of our lives, it's time to work out how to get there. Changes can be difficult, and during any process like this it can be hard to stay focused. It's easy to be thrown off course by unexpected obstacles, so we need something to keep us on track and heading firmly towards our own vision of success.

In the business community, this is normally the cue for some bright spark to start working up a hefty strategy document, complete with charts, graphics, lengthy arguments and who knows what. Before you knew it, you'd have a 50-page brick of a document that would be so off-putting that it would immediately be put on the shelf. And there it would stay.

No, it doesn't matter whether your goal is to be the head of a company with a £10 million turnover or whether you are simply looking for a more fulfilling job; there is a better way. That better way is a one-page transition map that will be your guide on this journey. A transition map is your road map of how to get from A to B – from your current state to your future state, or personal vision of success. Figure 1 shows a blank version of this map, to help you get started. It may look a bit daunting now, but don't worry. We will be filling this map in throughout this book on a step-by-step basis and, as you progress through the process logically, all will become clear. The beauty of this one-page strategy is that it can be pinned to the wall, stuck on a fridge or used as a screen saver, and thus stay in constant sight as you begin this exciting journey towards the successful you.

For copies of the transition map template, visit my website: www.mikeg-reene.co.uk/tmt.

If it helps, think about the transition map in terms of a real map. Imagine you want to get from, say, London to Scotland, and need to ask for directions. The first thing you need to explain is where you are now, because no one can plan a route until they know the starting point. That's your current state. The second thing you need to do is to specify more precisely where you would like to be. 'Scotland' is not very accurate. Do you mean Glasgow or Aberdeen? There is a difference of 122 miles between these cities, so being more specific will save you a lot of time later on.

**Current State**

There is a lovely old Irish saying that goes something like 'if I wanted to get there, I wouldn't start from here!' Sadly, though, we are all saddled with our 'here' and, like it or not, that is our starting point. All we can do is accept it and work out how to reach our vision.

So, let's begin with an appraisal of your current state.

The key here is to be *honest*! It is human nature to always try to make the outside world believe that things are going better than they actually are. But it is vitally important that you are 100 per cent accurate in your appraisal of your current state. Looking at it in terms of the taxi analogy in the above exercise, if you give your driver the wrong address to pick you up from, he won't ever find you and you will be stymied from the beginning. It's best to get everything into the open from the outset for a smooth journey. If you want to be four stone lighter, have £4 million in the bank or have happy kids and a good relationship, you need to be utterly honest about just how far you are from this ideal right now.

For the sake of illustration, I am going to look at two different types of transition. One is a transformation of a personal situation and the other is more applicable to someone running a business. The two transitions will run as a theme throughout the book. You may be looking at completely different success goals, but the principles are the same and the examples here will set you off on the right road. (For more examples of completed transition maps, visit my website at www.mikegreene.co.uk/tm.)

Let's take the business example first. For this I will use a mythical inter-net company that I shall call Acme Web Corp (AWC).

Looking at the books of AWC, I can see that it is a moderately success-ful – although not particularly inspiring – company. It has a turnover of £6 million, with a profit margin of 14 per cent. It has debts of £1 million and

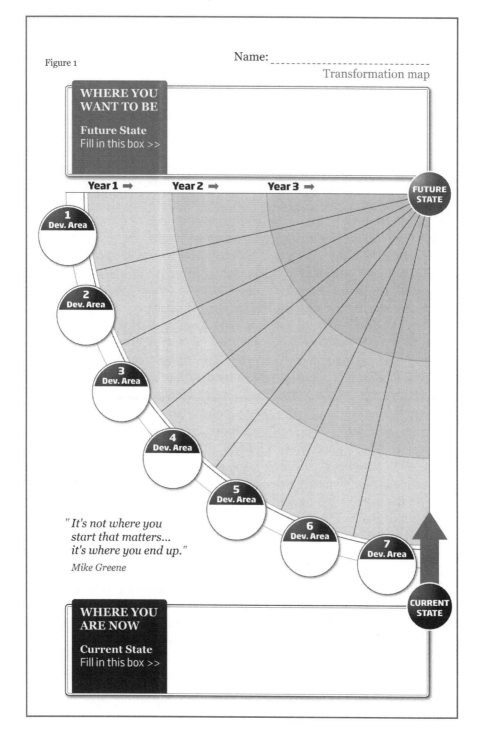

Figure 1

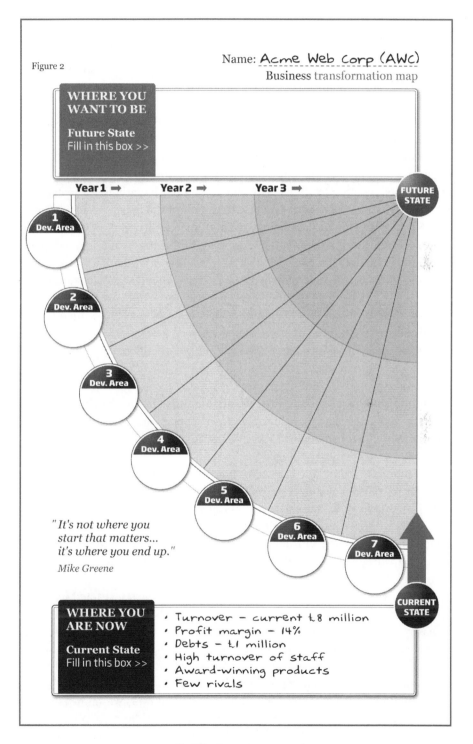

Figure 2

Name: _Acme Web Corp (AWC)_
Business transformation map

**WHERE YOU WANT TO BE**

**Future State**
Fill in this box >>

Year 1 ⇒    Year 2 ⇒    Year 3 ⇒    FUTURE STATE

1 Dev. Area
2 Dev. Area
3 Dev. Area
4 Dev. Area
5 Dev. Area
6 Dev. Area
7 Dev. Area

CURRENT STATE

_"It's not where you start that matters... it's where you end up."_
Mike Greene

**WHERE YOU ARE NOW**

**Current State**
Fill in this box >>

• Turnover — current £8 million
• Profit margin — 14%
• Debts — £1 million
• High turnover of staff
• Award-winning products
• Few rivals

an unusually high turnover of staff. On the plus side, it has won awards for some of its key products and has very few rivals in its particular sector.

Looking at your own situation, summarise the key points of your current state and insert them into your transition map. The 'current state' section in AWC's transition map is shown in Figure 2.

Now, let's consider the alternative scenario, which includes more personal goals. To begin with, take a long, hard look at your current state.

For the sake of our example, our personal-transition guinea pig is 'Joe'. Figure 3 shows his current state. Joe works as a junior manager in a supermarket, a job he fell into after school and doesn't particularly like. He earns £20,000 a year, but has never saved a penny and tries to ignore his mounting credit-card debt, which now stands at £5000. He is 30 years old and still lives at home with his parents, and has done little exercise throughout his twenties. He is unfit and two stone overweight. He has few hobbies to speak of and spends his free time playing *Call of Duty* on the Xbox. Joe has had a few on–off relationships over the years, but has never met anyone particularly special. At the back of his mind, though, he does yearn to settle down, marry and have children. The time just never seems right.

Now we must consider how we want to change our outlook.

**Future state**

The future state is, of course, what we are aiming to get to. Having set out your vision of success, now is the time to articulate what this will mean in real terms. Imagine yourself in three years time. What will you be doing? How could your life have changed?

Be ambitious. After all, hopefully you have some pretty lofty goals in mind for your vision of success. Don't get bogged down by your current view of reality. Remember, the sheer process of planning and of writing down your goals will have a multiplier effect and accelerate your progress. Doing something like this will substantially reduce the amount of time it will take you to get where you want to be. What would have been a five- or six-year plan could be reduced to just two or three years.

It's also useful to remind yourself that reality is always restricted by the time frame of today. Thus, if you were asked today what car you would drive if money were no object, you might say a Mercedes C Class – if you don't have a car or have one that's older or cheaper, that's a great one to have. But, as you became more successful, it is quite likely that if you were asked the same question you'd plump for a Ferrari!

When Julia and I were at rock bottom and bankrupt, we often talked about how, if we worked hard and saved, we might one day have a bank ac

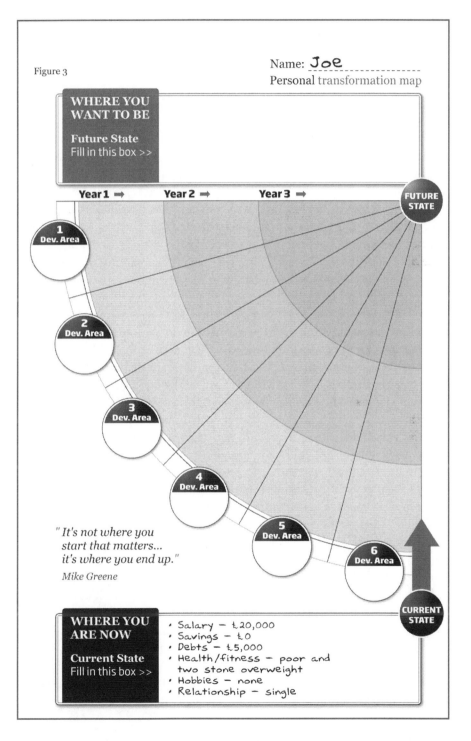

Figure 3

Name: **Joe**
Personal transformation map

**WHERE YOU WANT TO BE**

**Future State**
Fill in this box >>

Year 1 ⇒     Year 2 ⇒     Year 3 ⇒     FUTURE STATE

1 Dev. Area
2 Dev. Area
3 Dev. Area
4 Dev. Area
5 Dev. Area
6 Dev. Area

CURRENT STATE

*"It's not where you start that matters... it's where you end up."*
Mike Greene

**WHERE YOU ARE NOW**

**Current State**
Fill in this box >>

- Salary — £20,000
- Savings — £0
- Debts — £5,000
- Health/fitness — poor and two stone overweight
- Hobbies — none
- Relationship — single

fbs@mikegreene.co.uk

count once more, and perhaps a small mortgage on a cottage. That was our goal and, in the situation we were then in, it was a pretty big one! The reality was, as we moved along the journey, our vision widened and we started to think about owning seven or eight houses. Looking back now, I should have put this in my 'future state' section then. It was, after all, achievable – as I have proved.

If you still feel uneasy about seeing things from an ambitious perspective, take a leap of faith. Indulge yourself by dreaming for a while, because you will soon start to feel differently as you work through this book. Trust me – it will be worth it.

Make it a broad vision, too, because if you only consider one or two areas of your life, you won't have a proper, long-lasting solution. For example, if you run a business and your vision of your future state is to double your sales, due consideration must be given to what is supporting that aim. If the company has a shaky financial structure, is reliant on too few clients or has no proper legal framework, the super new turnover will mean nothing because it will be part of a really unstable business. You may never be able to sell that business because the few clients you do have might leave at any time because the contracts you have with them are not rock solid. Or, you could be hit with a massive tax bill that you have not planned for because the accounting processes are not built on a solid foundation.

If your vision of success is more personal, the same principles apply. Say that your goal is to be super-fit and slim, with an amazing home life. If the only way you could manage this would screw up your job because you would always have to be going in late to work after putting in some hard hours at the gym, that wouldn't work in the long term either.

The whole point of a transition map is to understand the areas you need to improve on, think about what the specific improvements should be and make sure you grow *all* those improvements simultaneously. Figure 4 shows some ambitious goals for the accelerated growth of AWC. To add a sense of urgency to the mix, my vision of success for AWC is to sell it at the end of year three, realising the greatest possible price.

In the case of Joe, our personal transition case study, I have been equally ambitious. As you will see in Figure 5, Joe is aiming to triple his salary over a three-year period. This will help him with his next two aims, which are to build up savings of £20,000 and clear his credit-card debts. Joe is also planning to change his personal situation by getting fit, shedding his excess weight and taking up at least two new hobbies. The turnaround in his fortunes will be complete when he meets and marries his dream woman.

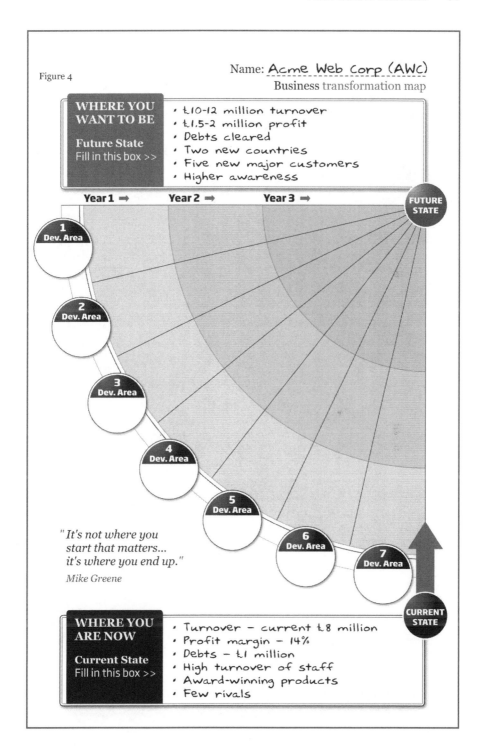

Figure 4

Name: Acme Web Corp (AWC)

Business transformation map

**WHERE YOU WANT TO BE**

**Future State**
Fill in this box >>

- £10-12 million turnover
- £1.5-2 million profit
- Debts cleared
- Two new countries
- Five new major customers
- Higher awareness

Year 1 ➡  Year 2 ➡  Year 3 ➡  FUTURE STATE

1 Dev. Area
2 Dev. Area
3 Dev. Area
4 Dev. Area
5 Dev. Area
6 Dev. Area
7 Dev. Area

CURRENT STATE

"It's not where you start that matters... it's where you end up."
Mike Greene

**WHERE YOU ARE NOW**

**Current State**
Fill in this box >>

- Turnover – current £8 million
- Profit margin – 14%
- Debts – £1 million
- High turnover of staff
- Award-winning products
- Few rivals

fbs@mikegreene.co.uk

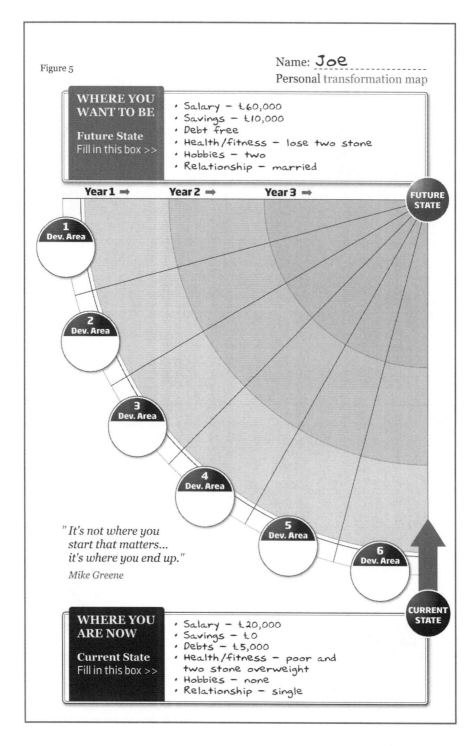

Figure 5

Name: **Joe**
Personal transformation map

**WHERE YOU WANT TO BE**

**Future State**
Fill in this box >>

- Salary — £60,000
- Savings — £10,000
- Debt free
- Health/fitness — lose two stone
- Hobbies — two
- Relationship — married

Year 1 ⇒    Year 2 ⇒    Year 3 ⇒    FUTURE STATE

1 Dev. Area
2 Dev. Area
3 Dev. Area
4 Dev. Area
5 Dev. Area
6 Dev. Area

CURRENT STATE

*"It's not where you start that matters... it's where you end up."*
Mike Greene

**WHERE YOU ARE NOW**

**Current State**
Fill in this box >>

- Salary — £20,000
- Savings — £0
- Debts — £5,000
- Health/fitness — poor and two stone overweight
- Hobbies — none
- Relationship — single

If you have started your own transition map, congratulations! We now know what success will look like for you. If you haven't, make time to do one. Don't put it off – the sooner you begin, the sooner you will realise your goals.

By writing down your vision, you've made a subconscious contract with yourself. You've set your ambitions in stone, as it were, and this is so much more effective than a few muttered 'I wish I hads' or 'I would always have loved tos'. Now your future is mapped out, and if you ignore your plan you will have to live with yourself every day when you look in the mirror.

In the following chapters, I will show you how to travel from your current state to that future state. There are many different options for how to do this. To return to our map analogy, you could choose to take the train, drive, fly or even walk to Scotland. Each of the options has its own strengths and limitations. By analogy, as we go through the exercise, you may decide that a three-year plan requires more effort than you are prepared, or are able, to give. You may be comfortable with a five-year plan. Alternatively, you may be in a tearing hurry and prepared to sacrifice everything in a fast-track journey to your goals, and decide to aim to complete them in a year. The choice is yours. The decision you will have to make at some point soon is what price you are prepared to pay in inconvenience, pain and personal commitment to make it all happen. What's important is that you go at a pace you are comfortable with and don't get discouraged.

To give yourself one final boost, as we close this chapter, why not share your transition map with someone you trust? I've always rather liked the old adage that you can be hung by your tongue. In this case, this basically means that, if you articulate your goals to someone, you are more likely to make them happen. After all, if you tell your pals that you are going to lose two stone in weight and they see you eating a Big Mac, they may just ask what happened to your diet. Having aired your vision, knowing that this sort of negative feedback is a possibility will add further momentum to your quest.

Apart from anything else, by just saying what you want to achieve out loud, you will get a massive and immediate sense of what it will be like when you do make it happen. You will be able to breathe in your vision of success and almost taste what it will be like when you reach your goal. Defining your vision of success is a very important first step to turning around your life. Instead of crossing your fingers and hoping the future will be better, you now know with certainty that it will be so.

So, let's get on with making it happen.

Finally, there is a quote (unattributed) I have always been rather motivated by, and it might give you a boost too: 'Write it down. Written goals have a way of transforming wishes into wants; can'ts into cans; dreams into plans; and plans into reality. Don't just think it – ink it!'

## QUICK EXERCISE

### Think, believe, dream, dare

I'd like to share with you a piece of writing I did in the summer of 2001. At the time, I had virtually nothing. Although, through sheer hard work and determination, Julia and I had managed to buy our first house after the bankruptcy, I still wasn't really sure how I would ever achieve my long-held dream of becoming a millionaire. It certainly didn't seem much of a possibility in the position I was then in. But, undeterred, I used up what little savings I had to go on a motivational seminar. While I was there, the speaker asked us to visualise our lives 20 years hence. This is an extract from what I wrote.

*I wake up each day and have to pinch myself to believe what a wonderfully amazing life I have. I can smell the delicious breakfast being cooked by the housekeeper. As I open my eyes, I see Julia looking beautiful and re-laxed and I can hear the birds singing and children playing. These are my grandchildren because my daughter Rosie has come to stay with us for a few weeks. Our house is a beautiful Victorian farmhouse which we have developed over the years and to which we have added the gym, pool and leisure complex.*

*I decide not to work today, as I have a great team who are more than able to develop and grow my business without me. Julia and I decide to have a swim. The pool is always kept at a comfortable temperature and I love starting the day with a swim, sauna and Jacuzzi before breakfast. After breakfast, we decide that as Rosie is stopping for a few days, we should all go to the house in Monaco for the weekend and so I go to telephone our pilot to get the plane fuelled and ready for departure.*

I confess that, until recently, I had forgotten all about the existence of this document. I discovered it when I was clearing out some papers in my office, after I had sold my company in late 2011. Reading it through, I was amazed.

This is my life now, I thought.

Barring a few details – I don't have a private plane, for example – I have achieved this luxurious dream. I articulated my goals and they happened.

The philosophy behind this idea follows an experiment credited to Harvard Business School in which only 3 per cent of the graduating class had specific written goals for their futures. Twenty years later, that 3 per cent was found to be earning ten times the amount of their old classmates who had no clear goals. As it turns out, this study is an urban myth, but it has since been emulated by Dominican University and there is now empirical evidence to prove the effectiveness of writing down one's goals.[1] The study found an almost 50 per cent improvement in just a month following written goals – imagine what you could achieve over three or more years!

So, dare to dream. Take a sheet of A4 and write down where you will be and what you will be doing in 20 years' time. Writing down your goals is one of the most important actions you can take towards obtaining the life – and success – you want.

1 See, for example, http://cdn.sidsavara.com/wp-content/uploads/2008/09/research-summary2.pdf.

## Summary

- Write down your desired future outcome, being as broad as possible.
- Think big.
- Write down your current situation, being as thorough as possible (but be honest – don't sugar-coat it).
- Once you have your future state or vision of success, involve other people who can motivate you and discipline you when you waver.

## ADDITIONAL PPA EXERCISE

In the introduction to this book, I identified the four Personal Profile Analysis (PPA) personality groups, which are described in terms of four key factors: dominance, influence, steadiness and compliance. If you chose to identify your own profile by completing the questionnaire on my website, the following additional information, which is specifically tailored to the personality types, will give you some clues to understand how you are reacting to what you have read so far and how you may best use this chapter for your own style of thinking and learning.

### Dominance messages
- Writing down your future state in detail makes it explicit; it will act as a spur along the way.
- Don't let false realism limit your ambition.
- Describe your current state honestly and accurately.
- Other people can add value to your project, but only if you let them.

### Influence messages
- Engage your optimism to formulate the dream of your future state.
- Be specific.
- Describe your current state, warts and all, without gloss.
- Choose people to help you who will not just tell you what you want to hear.

### Steadiness messages
- To create the best and most secure future for yourself, aim high.
- Standing still is not an option, so embrace change.
- The transition-map tool is your safety net.
- Elicit support from those who can help you along the way.

### Compliance messages
- Identify only the key elements in your current situation and desired future state so that excessive detail does not distract from the major objectives.
- Follow the structured plan inherent in the transition map.
- Choose a trusted person to challenge you when necessary.

## CHAPTER TWO

## DON'T ACCEPT LABELS

The greatest wisdom is to know thyself – The Talmud

Even after I was made bankrupt in my mid-twenties thanks to a disastrous series of events, I still had my long-held dream of becoming a millionaire. At that time, the goal seemed a million miles away and about as obtainable as flying to the moon. That didn't make me change my ambitions, though. Thus, while delivering pizzas for a friend in order to make ends meet, I threw myself into reading – because, after all, knowledge from books is free. I also instinctively felt that books might hold some clues as to how I could get myself out of the mess I had got into and closer to my goals and dreams.

One of the first books I read on my quest for enlightenment was *Live Your Dreams* by Les Brown.[2] In this tale of personal growth, one of the stories that most resonated with me was about Brown's school years. Early on in his life, Brown had been labelled 'educationally retarded' by the American school system. The label basically dismissed him at a stroke and declared that he was one who would never achieve very much, if anything at all.

---

2. Les Brown, *Live Your Dreams*. William Morrow, 1994.

One day, a new teacher came to Brown's class and in the course of the lesson she asked him to answer a question.

Brown told the teacher that he was sorry – he didn't know. Then, sensing that perhaps this was not enough, he added the explanation that he was 'educationally retarded'.

The teacher picked up a board rubber and threw it straight at him.

Looking genuinely shocked and angry, she told him that he was not a label. She urged him never, ever, to accept someone else's label.

At the time that I was reading this story, I was as close to rock bottom as it is possible to be. I did not have a penny to my name and all my official records showed very clearly that I was a 'bankrupt'. I wasn't allowed to borrow money without telling the lender I was a bankrupt. I wasn't allowed to act as a director of a company. I certainly wasn't allowed to manage a business without telling anyone concerned that I was a bankrupt. In fact, the word 'bankrupt' was everywhere I looked and that eight-letter label dominated my life.

Suddenly, though, after reading Les Brown's story about how he went on to triumph over his negative label and find success beyond his or anyone's dreams and expectations, I realised I didn't have to be 'a bankrupt'. I didn't have to define myself and every aspect of my life by that horrible moniker. I didn't have to wear a shirt with bankrupt emblazoned across the front and go around with my head bowed in shame. I didn't have to project my apparent disgrace and struggle in everything I did. All I was doing by adopting this negative attitude was heaping more harm on an already poor situation.

If, on the other hand, I accepted and embraced what had happened and took time to understand the lessons I had learned, I would immediately be in a far stronger position.

This important moment was the trigger that got me back on my feet and fighting once again. Just by mentally shedding the bankruptcy label that had haunted me for months, I felt better. Almost overnight I grew as a person. I could see light at the end of the very dark tunnel I had been trapped in for far too long.

We are all guilty of accepting labels. We all believe we are too uneducated, or too overweight, or too badly trained, or too depressed, or too something else to be a success, to be loved or to belong. If I asked you now what your label is, you'd probably be able to tell me straight away. If not, try answering the following questions:

*Deep down inside, I am not good enough because....'*

*or*

*'I could do so much better if....'*

And, guess what, while you think like this, you probably are not good enough! We, as human beings, are only able to see the world through the eyes we are looking through at any given moment. We project our negative labels into everything we do and this has a real effect on the outcome. If you *believe* you are not good enough, then you *won't be* good enough.

Added to this is the fact that around 70 per cent of human communication takes place through nonverbal cues. We communicate in the way we look at another person, whether we maintain eye contact and even in the way we stand. Often it is more about the way we say things, rather than what we say in itself. People subconsciously read these clues and, if their subconscious doesn't like what they see (even if they don't realise why), there will be a lack of trust. When this happens, it is harder than ever to get things done.

The way you view yourself really does make a difference.

With this in mind, I always play a little game with myself to predict the outcome of sporting events and political debates. My high accuracy rate is all the more uncanny, because very often I know quite little about the teams and personalities involved. But, as soon as I hear the principal say something like 'well, it's going to be tough but we'll do our best', I know they are stuffed and will lose horribly. It's the team that says confidently that they are great and are going to win, no argument, that will triumph. It's true. My 'win-o-meter' is right almost every time. Try it yourself!

Believing you are going to win, or be a success, or will lose weight, doesn't mean you will automatically go on to do so, but add in a bit of effort and action behind that self-confidence and your chances will increase exponentially. In contrast, if you don't believe you will triumph, you certainly won't. After all, returning to the taxi-driver analogy in chapter one, your driver will only ever be able to take you where you tell him to go. And, as the great man Nelson Mandela once said, 'The greatest glory in living lies not in never falling, but in rising every time we fail.'

The way we label ourselves is a destination. We all have a choice about the way we look at things and, if we are not prepared to be positive, our negative labels will define us for the rest of our lives. Recognise your negative labels and get out from under them.

### Where our labels come from

None of us started out life with these labels. When a child is just two or three years old, he believes he can be anything he wants to be and that everything is possible. Give a kid a stick and instantly he is a soldier, or a pretty dress and straight away she is a beautiful princess. At this age there are no barriers to their confidence or self-belief.

So, somewhere along the way, our limiting beliefs creep in. But where and how?

To be fair, this label issue is not solely your fault. Many of our most negative views of ourselves were drummed into us by others at an early age. If, for example, as a lad Pete's parents repeatedly said that 'little Pete is not very good at sports', pretty soon, little Pete will not be good at sports. He will give up trying because, as we all know and Pete certainly does, parents know everything. Similarly, if Kate's parents continually declare that she is clumsy and that, if there is a glass in the room she will invariably knock it over, pretty soon she will do so every time. It will be programmed into her and she will barely be able to help herself living up to everyone's view of her.

Look at this in scientific terms. Our amazing brains process 100 million bits of information per second. Around 98 per cent of that is deleted by the reticular activating system (the part of the brain that, as well as sorting everything out, acts like a giant filter to get rid of things deemed to be unnecessary). Of the 2 million or so pieces of information that remain, your brain only allows up to ten to surface to your conscious awareness. This is how decisions are made, memories are burned and situations are experienced. This is why Kate is vulnerable to what is being highlighted about her again and again. It is not that she is clumsy, but that the suggestion that she is clumsy is so prevalent in her consciousness that pretty soon she won't be able to stop thinking she is.

It's like if I say to you now: don't think of pink elephants, don't think of pink elephants, don't think of pink elephants. I bet you are thinking of a large, rosy-coloured mammal with large ears and a trunk right now!

'But,' you may be thinking, 'my parents were encouraging but I was rubbish at school. I got the worst marks in every test and my end-of-term reports were a sea of Ds and Es.' That doesn't mean you are stupid, though, or destined for the scrap heap. Remember, schools have very tight parameters in their teaching. By its very nature, the majority of the education system is one size fits all and is entirely focused on getting youngsters through exams. It's rather like the way that we receive instruction in order to pass our driving tests and yet the majority of us actually learn to drive after we've got our license. Teachers work to a tight curriculum have a definite view of how children should respond. It doesn't take much to fall outside the accepted limits. It's easy to be sidelined, written off or ignored if you don't fit in. The thing to remember, though, is that it is never too late to shed a label.

I myself was regularly dismissed as a naughty, scruffy kid at school and constantly scolded for not conforming. A lot of teachers couldn't see beyond that label – which they themselves had given me – despite the fact that beneath all the bluff, bravado and scruffiness I was actually a pretty bright child. Luckily for me, I was driven and ambitious enough to get out from under the label I had been given and see it for what it was. I know a lot of people struggle with this, though. A teacher is in a tremendously powerful position and, just as a good teacher can be the making of a child, a bad (or short sighted) one can destroy a child too.

In chapter eight I will talk more about dealing with our 'pack' – the friends, family, teachers and colleagues we surround ourselves with as we go through life. But it is important to point out now that, most of the time, the harmful things these people say are not malicious or intentional. Most of the time they mean the best. They think they are being helpful, even though in reality they are the opposite. Then, we do the rest ourselves. Very often, we subconsciously make up our own labels in response to things we don't understand, or that trouble us, or that make us feel vulnerable. We add in our own homemade 'because' to the 'I don't feel good enough' question to help us better fit in. For example, if a person doesn't get a job they want and need, they might blame their own skills or intelligence, whereas there may be a million other reasons why they didn't succeed that time, and 99.9 per cent of those reasons will be nothing to do with the person's competency or suitability for the post.

Whatever their source, the bad news is that you will not be able to shed these labels overnight or immediately forget them and move on. The problem with these negative, or limiting, beliefs is that, once they get locked into your mind and the longer they are locked in there, the deeper they will go, even if there is no longer any evidence to support them. There is no magic exercise to rid you of these negative beliefs. However unfounded or unreasonable, they became part of you long ago and are hard-wired in your brain. Just as you never truly forget anything you have ever seen, heard or done, you can't simply erase them from your memory.

However, you can *accept* the past and those limiting beliefs, and ensure that they don't define you in the future. Your past doesn't have to be who you are and definitely doesn't have to be who you become. Furthermore, it can become a very solid experiential foundation on which to build. After all, as the saying goes, if it doesn't kill you, it makes you stronger.

It is time to ditch those labels.

### Fly like a bumblebee

Back in the 1930s, scientists apparently proved that bumblebees cannot fly, declaring that, because they are large insects with small, rigid wings, they shouldn't be able to get airborne. Yet there it is, every summer, the humble

*Bombus terristris*, buzzing around from flower to flower. Clearly no one told the bumble bee it was not technically able to do this.

History is littered with stories of people who have succeeded against all the odds. Take a tour of the biography section of your local library and you will be able to read tale after tale of people who have achieved things that technically they should never have been able to do. I've no doubt that along the way most of them encountered naysayers who said what they were attempting was not possible. I'm sure they were told 'you'll never be good enough to do that' more than once.

But they did it anyway.

They have proved that, if you ignore those negative labels that people keep trying to give you, and if you believe, you can be whatever you want to be. It is all about accepting responsibility for yourself and your future.

---

## QUICK EXERCISE

### Weed or flower?

While you are pondering the labels you have acquired over the years, set aside a moment to take a deep breath and smell the roses – or whichever flower you can lay your hands on. Then consider for a moment what you would define as a flower and what you would call a weed. I'll place a strong bet that each reader will have a different view.

Some people, for example, adore the humble dandelion, loving its array of bright yellow petals arranged in perfect concentric circles. Fans may even tell you of the flower's amazing success in curing stomach problems or appendicitis, or eliminating acne. Others, though, see dandelions only as an annoying eyesore of a weed.

Neither group is right or wrong. Beauty is, of course, in the eye of the beholder. The point is: people may find beauty in something that others have derisively dismissed. If you extend this philosophy to the negative labels you are labouring under, perhaps there is an argument that you are simply not looking at things in the most positive way.

Perhaps you need to start seeing flowers instead of weeds.

---

I often say to the people that I mentor that the most exciting and yet also the most scary phrase that you can ever hear is: you are in control of your own future. Yes, when you accept that it is not someone else's responsibility to support your endeavours, boost your confidence or give you food, money or shelter, that is the moment that the world is your oyster. As soon as you stop blaming your parents, your school, your boss or the government for not smoothing the way or encouraging you, your life will change completely. The possibilities of what you can achieve are endless.

Now, you may be reading this and thinking 'but my mum and dad always told me I was a useless waster – it's hard to get over that'. My answer is: yes, you've had a raw deal, but get over it! You are an adult and perfectly capable of telling yourself that you are not useless.

Better still, turn that negative label into a strength!

There is a great saying that springs to mind here: get off your butt. It doesn't translate so well to the written word, but if you say it out loud it can be taken in two ways. First, it means 'get off your backside and do some-thing'. It also means 'stop using the word *but*' – as in, 'I would love to do so and so, *but…*'. Your life is in your hands. Don't waste it.

Believe it or not, for everyone who believes their life has been blighted by problems at home, school or at work, there is another person who uses the same kinds of experiences to stiffen their resolve and make them a better person.

Imagine, for example, a child who was bought up by an alcoholic parent. If he too turned to drink in his adulthood, he may very well say: 'What do you expect? My father was an alcoholic. It's all I've ever known.'

Another child, bought up in almost identical circumstances, might say something very different. She may say that she has done everything she could to strive to be successful because, after seeing how low her father could go, she vowed she would never be like that: 'My father was a bum,' she might say. 'There was no way I could ever end up like he did.'

Two children with the same upbringing, the same conditioning and the same labels, but with vastly differing outcomes.

One of my comedic heroes, Billy Connolly, has spoken movingly about the sexual and physical abuse he suffered as a child at the hands of his father.[3] He was also subjected to harrowing attacks by his aunt Mona, who regularly beat him with wet cloths, or kicked and pounded him on the head with the heel of her shoe. An upbringing like this could easily have de-stroyed anyone and saddled them with more debilitating labels than it is possible to imagine, yet Connolly rose above all of this. Indeed, he has made a career out of seeing the funny side of awkward situations, which has won him the adoration of tens of thousands of fans.

---

3. Pamela Stephenson, *Billy*. HarperCollins, 2001.

It is possible to do the impossible and rise above the labels we have endured all our lives. You just have to make the decision to do so.

## Fake it till you make it!

How daft, you may be thinking. What's the point of me declaring that I am brilliant and that one day I will be a millionaire, while I am working in a dead-end job, living in rotten accommodation and hardly have a penny to my name?

Well, we've all got to start somewhere!

A great first step is to decide to shed the labels and aim high. If you accept that you need to take action, you will get there quicker, I guarantee it. You do have to believe it, though. You can say 'I'm going to be a millionaire, I'm going to be a millionaire, I'm going to be a millionaire' as many times as you like, but, if you are down in the dumps and held back by your negative labels, it is not likely to happen.

There are plenty of other practical measures that you can use to help you get out from under your labels. One of the easiest things to do is to look more closely at the source of these negative beliefs. Now you have taken the trouble to define what your limiting beliefs are, it is but a small step to discredit the source of these labels.

Imagine for a moment that perhaps the person (or people) who gave you the label was never really qualified to do so. Thus, concerned parents who urgently try to steer their child away from her ambition to be a rock star and try to encourage her into a 'safer', more dependable career (such as banking) may not be the most unbiased advisors. Yes, they probably take their stance out of a position of love and concern that their child does not experience any disappointment or failure, but how much do they really know about the music business? Unless the parents have names like Adele, Sting, Peter Gabriel or Ozzy Osbourne, maybe they are a little outside their comfort zone. Sure, if their ambitious would-be rocker offspring were to be told by a dozen rock stars and the same number of studio talent scouts that she was tone deaf, then a change of ambition may be in order. The point is, though, that none of us should let our dreams go simply because people who are not qualified to give advice stick their two penn'orth in.

Looking back at my childhood declaration that one day I would be a millionaire, I still thank my lucky stars that my mother could not have been more encouraging. Never once did she say 'what are you talking about, Mike, don't be so daft!' But, if she had scoffed at my lofty visions, I hope I would have had the strength of mind to have realised that she was not really the right person to judge whether or not I could attain this goal. Despite a

## QUICK EXERCISE

### Quick exercise

Cancel the pity party

If I ever came home crying after a scuffle at school, my mother always gave me pretty short shrift.

'Did you fight back?' she would demand. A sharp and painful cuff to my ear would usually accompany the phrase.

Thus, I learned at a very early age that expecting the consolation and comfort of a pitying embrace (or indulging in 'pity parties', as they became known in my household) really wasn't very productive. Sooner or later, I resolved that I would no longer indulge myself with any pity parties as they never really got me anywhere. To be honest, I may have gone a bit too far in the wrong direction and can sometimes be a bit brutal to friends who come to me with tales of woe.

'Yes, that's tough,' I say. 'But, compared with some of the other things that are going on in the world, is it really as big a deal as you are making it out to be?'

This may seem harsh, but why don't you try this exercise on yourself? Next time you are feeling sorry for yourself and setting up for a nice pity party, stop for a moment and ask yourself some honest (really honest) questions. Do you have a reason to be feeling that bad? Is this the worst thing that has ever happened to you? Has what has happened to distress you left you in constant physical pain?

The answers will probably be no, no and no. So, stop feeling sorry for yourself, don't let the negativity get you down (whether it is self-induced or forced upon you by others) and get on with your life.

In short – look on the bright side and be positive!

wealth of other admirable qualities, she had not been rich or successful in her career. She was not in a position to judge or saddle me with a limiting belief.

By discrediting these sources of negative labels, I don't mean you must cast them off, or never speak to them again. Some of the people who have shaped your personality are, of course, close family and friends. There is no way that you should even consider turning your back on them. That would be cruel and rude. However, what you can begin to do is to analyse why they gave you the labels that they did and in your own mind discredit their reasons for doing so.

## Scratch your negative CD

Very often, people hold on to their negative labels intentionally. They find comfort in playing back their bad memories again and again, as though the memories were a soundtrack CD or DVD on a constant loop. In fact, they revel in it! The moment an opportunity for a pity party begins and it looks like there might be an opening for some sympathy, kind words or attention from others, they can call up their sad memory and be miserable on demand.

I've seen this situation a hundred times. Quite recently, for example, I spoke to a man who obviously couldn't wait to tell me that his life was a mess.

'Why's that?' I asked.

'Well, I lost both my parents and then my wife. I have been left to bring up my children on my own,' he said, shaking his head in apparent abject misery. 'As a result of all this, my career is a mess and I have to really struggle to make ends meet.'

Yet, delving further into his tale, it turned out that his sad loss had happened seven years earlier, his children were teenagers on the brink of leaving home and he was in a good job earning £70,000 a year. Now, I don't want to sound callous, because it is of course a tragedy to lose loved ones, but it seemed to me that this man had an awful lot going for him and far more to be grateful for than he was acknowledging. His entire psyche was stuck in 2005, the year he saw his life going off the rails, and he seemed to be holding on to this feeling like grim death. Clearly, he had etched his sad story onto his personal CD seven years before, at a time when he was probably surrounded by sympathetic relatives, yet he had never subsequently shed the need for the comfort of others' pity. He simply couldn't move on. In his mind, he was stuck in a never-ending loop in which he felt compelled to replay his CD to summon up the tears so that people would give him the sorrowful looks he so desired. It was his crutch and his way of getting attention.

I told him that the only way he could move on and get on with his life was to scratch that CD, so it could never be played again, and find a new, more positive tune. That would be the only way he would ever find true happiness once more and see that his life was in fact filled with good things.

Scratching that CD can be as easy as acknowledging to yourself that you have been relying on your negative feelings or labels as a crutch. Perhaps if you are honest with yourself you may realise that you've been using them as an excuse not to take some action or do something potentially daunting.

This is not to say that you should endeavour to forget the painful memory or negative labels. You shouldn't do that – and you couldn't, because it will be hard-wired into your brain. Indeed, the ability to remember and interpret emotional events from the past is what forms the basic foundation of our personalities. What you need to do is to understand what has happened in your past and learn from it, without letting it be something that will define your life forever. You need to confront the memory or label and reframe it in your mind.

Talking to someone about what happened and how you feel about it can help you to come to terms with bad memories or negative labels (although don't fall into the trap of the man mentioned above, who had been talking about his memories for seven years and never moved on). Writing it down in a diary or journal can be very therapeutic too. Airing your fears and upsets will go a long way to helping you understand that this experience was not your fault and was probably completely beyond your control. In fact, although your experience may always have been painful to think about, it may hold some useful lessons. It could, for example, make you a stronger person because you will see that you have survived it. You may come to feel that, if you can survive whatever it is that is disturbing you, you can withstand anything.

Now is the time to let all the negativity behind this label go and to be at peace.

There are, of course, more drastic options for wiping clean your personal CD. I once saw an example, done to great effect, at an Tony Robbins seminar. The legendary life coach was talking to a large man who had confessed that his long-term addiction to chocolate was making his life a misery and was ruining his health. Robbins listened patiently and finally asked this chap whether he was prepared to let this addiction go on.

'You could go to counselling and it will take months if not years to rid you of this addiction and the negative feelings that have led to it, or I can help deal with it in an hour,' he said.

'OK,' agreed the large man.

That evening, the large man was called back onto the stage and Robbins produced a slab of raw belly pork and a large bar of chocolate. With a dramatic flourish, he rubbed the once pristine bar of milk chocolate all over with the raw pork fat. He then offered it to the chocolate addict and indicated that he should eat it. All credit to the chap: he reached out and took the chocolate and eventually ate it all up, even though he was retching all the way through. The audience in the seminar went mad cheering him on.

What an experience it was, though. The disgusting taste of that foul raw pork fat and the drama of the occasion succeeded in scratching this portly man's CD. The next day, when Robbins invited him up on stage and offered him a bar of luxury chocolate, the man refused and you could tell by his face that his addiction to the sweet stuff was well and truly over.

This is obviously an extreme way to scratch your CD and dispense with the kinds of negative memories we all hold on to. But, whatever method you choose, once you've done it, it will transform your life. Success always comes at a price – indeed, the only place where success appears before work is in the dictionary – but the effort will be worth your while. You will be amazed how good you feel if you only make yourself let go.

Try it!

### Thou shalt not kid thyself

Although much of this chapter has been taken up with finding out more about who you (and others) think you are, don't forget the other side of the equation: *who do you want to be?*

The most important driver to get you from where you are now to where you want to be in the future (and therefore away from those negative, and usually spurious, labels) is the desire to do something special with your life. Never lose sight of the fact that the destination is far, far more important than where you are and where you have been.

In all of this examination of the past, present and future, you need to be utterly honest. You must also constantly ask yourself whether you are prepared to pay the price of moving on and embracing the future you really deserve. This always brings to mind my own 11th commandment: *thou shalt not kid thyself.* No success comes without a price. Many of the things you have had to confront through this chapter will not have been easy to face, but it is only by facing them with utter truthfulness that you will be able to shed what holds you back and devote yourself to a successful future.

Returning to the transition map, which we began in chapter one, remember that you will not be able to make the journey from your current state to your desired future state until you know exactly where you are setting out from. After all, no one can direct you from one place to another unless they know where you are starting from.

Tackling some of what we have covered here may seem awkward, even uncomfortable, but in the following chapters I will show you how to channel all of these feelings into your journey forward. Now you have accepted that you are what you are, you are perfectly placed to take the next step in your own transition map.

Finally, if you are still harbouring any doubts at this stage, allow me to add one further proof that this transition is not just possible but that it can and will change your life. At the outset of the chapter I mentioned that my goals seemed about as attainable as reaching the moon. Well, not only did I achieve and exceed my goals but also, since I started out, the situation has changed substantially regarding space travel. Virgin is now just one company that is planning space trips for civilians, which says to me that anything is possible. The sky, and even beyond that, is the limit. We are only ever held back by our own mental limitations.

**Summary**
- Believe in yourself.
- Renounce all negative labels and beliefs.
- Learn from negative experiences.
- Your past does not define your future.

If you want to explore your own limiting beliefs and labels, you may find it helpful to complete Thomas International's Trait Emotional Intelligence Questionnaire (TEIQ). You can access this via my website, www.mikegreene. co.uk/teiq, but please be aware that you would require a debrief from a trained practitioner because of the potential sensitivity of the issues raised.

## ADDITIONAL PPA EXERCISE

The following information will give you some clues to understand how you are reacting to what you have read so far, in accordance with your personality type. It also gives some ideas on how you may best use this chapter for your own style of thinking and learning.

### Dominance messages
- You can do anything you put your mind to.
- Negative labels and beliefs are a challenge; prove them wrong.
- Failure is the opportunity to try again with the benefit of hindsight.
- Your future starts now: make it happen.

### Influence messages
- You are the star in your own life story.
- Don't let a bad review from yesterday stop you dazzling tomorrow.
- Look for the positives even when things go wrong.

- The past is gone: focus on creating a brighter future.

**Steadiness messages**
- You don't have to be loud or pushy to be successful, so trust in your own dogged persistence.
- Take stock of any labels and discard those holding you back.
- A methodical review when things go wrong provides a solid platform for improvement.
- History can provide useful pointers but the future is not a repeat performance.

**Compliance messages**
- Have confidence that your logical attention to detail will keep you on track.
- Apply your logical judgement to disprove negative labels.
- Extract the key learning points from past errors to boost future performance.
- The past is a springboard, not a straitjacket.

## CHAPTER THREE

# WHEN THE STUDENT IS READY, THE TEACHER WILL APPEAR

If I have seen further, it is by standing on the shoulders of giants

– Isaac Newton

Although I was always pretty certain that I would be a millionaire one day, I confess that, early on, I really didn't have a clue where to start. In my heart of hearts, I knew I was being held back by my own lack of confidence in myself and my abilities. Then, as if out of nowhere, a mentor appeared.

This mentor came in the unlikely shape of my local newsagent, Les Hooper. He had been kind enough to give me a paper round when I was the tender age of 11 and had always been encouraging to me. Although I was a scruffy kid, without much going for me, he recognised that I always turned up on time and was always happy to go out and do my job, whatever the weather. Rain or shine, I never complained.

When I reached 14 years old, Les offered me a part-time Saturday job in his store. I was a little taken aback as I had not asked for the extra work, although I was very grateful for the opportunity. Without a doubt, the additional money this job would bring in would be a vital lifeline for me and my family, who had always struggled to make ends meet.

'Thank you,' I managed to stammer out, once I had got over my surprise. 'But why me?'

'Because I believe in you, Mike,' Les replied with a warm smile.

Even today, I can remember the feeling of pride and achievement these six words stirred up in me. I resolved then and there to work as hard as humanly possible for this man, to prove that he was not mistaken in his faith in me. And I did.

Working in Les's store, I learned much more than simply how to stack shelves, manage a stock room and use a cash till. My time at the store taught me about the value of good, honest hard graft. It became clear to me that, the more effort I put in, the more I gained from the experience and the more responsibility was bestowed upon me. Many of these lessons have been applied to my work in later life and I am still grateful for the opportunity Les gave me and the things he taught me.

Les was just the first, although (after my mum) arguably the most important, in a line of people who helped to me achieve what I have achieved. He was a powerful mentor and appeared just when I needed a helping hand. His timely intervention brings to mind the Zen saying that goes: 'when the student is ready, the teacher will appear'. It means, be open to those who would mentor you, for they will always come to you, usually when you need them the most.

When we reach rock bottom, there is almost always someone there to give us a helping hand, or to give us some kind or useful words to get us back on our feet. The trick is being ready to recognise these opportunities, grab them with both hands and learn everything you can from them. The way to keep moving forward in life is to recognise and build on the greatness and generosity of others.

It doesn't have to be a fellow human being who gives you a hand up, although there are often more willing and supportive helpers around than you may imagine. Help can come from physical objects too, such as books. When I was made bankrupt in my mid-twenties, I turned to my local library in my quest to get back on my feet. I consumed book after book in the biography section, from A through to Z, like a man possessed, reading endless stories of inspirational figures from the worlds of business, politics, psychology and sport. I wanted to know all their secrets about getting to the top and winning – and there they all were, in glorious black and white, just waiting for me to come along. Who could fail to be inspired by such stories given freely by the world's most powerful teachers?

The catalyst for this thirst for knowledge, or desire for change, often comes when people reach their lowest point. They suddenly know that they need to make a change if they are not to simply sink without trace and be permanently blighted by what has brought them so low.

What separates the men from the boys – or, more specifically, what singles out those who go on to be successful and turn their lives around – is a willingness to actively seek out new views and to put the work in. If you sit down and wait for the solution to come to you, you may never move on. (This brings to mind another lovely saying, this one Chinese: 'A man who stands on a mountain waiting for a crispy duck to fly in has a long wait.' It is not quite Zen, but you get the picture.)

No, there is little point idling while you wait for your partner, family or the authorities to somehow sense your plight and intervene. Often, others do not even realise that those close to them need any help, or they may have pressing problems of their own to deal with. Expecting those in a position of power – such as the government, local authorities or even an employer – to swoop in and change things is often pretty unrealistic too. If you want to avail yourself of the services of a mentor or teacher, and stand on the shoulders of those giants, you must seek them out and find out what they can offer you.

So far in this book, we've worked to understand what success means to you as an individual; we've examined and rejected the labels that we've been given (or given ourselves); and we've mentally become comfortable with the fact that the people who gave us these labels were probably not qualified to do so. Now that you are ready to embark on a journey, it is time to get into a place where others can help you along.

By picking up this book, you have already made a valuable first step by demonstrating that you are ready to change your fortunes. In this chapter, and those that follow, I will act as your mentor. However, I will also show you how to find others to help you in your journey into success, because, just as I did, you will need multiple mentors as you go through your transition.

### What can a mentor do for you?

Over the years, I have done quite a lot of mentoring. If I was to sum up in one sentence how I help my mentees, I would say: *I help people find what they are passionate about and then show them how they could achieve that goal.*

Mentoring can drastically increase your chances of success. Whether your mentor simply lets you know that someone believes in you (which can be a pretty powerful thing) or whether your mentor actively provides you with the tools you need to excel, having someone on board with experience will speed up your transition process exponentially.

In purely basic terms, mentors can help you clarify career or life goals and assist you in your journey through your transition plan as you move towards reaching those goals. They do this by sharing the insights and knowledge they have gained through their own achievements.

**Mentors will:**
- provide guidance based on their own past experiences of success and failure
- help you identify problems and possible solutions
- offer constructive feedback and support.

Mentors will give you the tools to get you from where you are now to where you want to be. Yet, while they'll show you how you could emulate what they have achieved, they won't tell you what to do in step-by-step detail. All they will be able to do is help you look at your situation from all sides, consider all your options and then let you decide for yourself which one path is the best. Remember, you are (or will be) the expert in your field and the role of the mentor is merely to ensure you realise your true potential.

There is, however, a word of caution to add here. If you work with a mentor, you must commit to them 100 per cent. You cannot pick and choose which parts of their advice to follow, dismissing other bits as daft or impossible to do. Think of it like visiting a doctor and being given a course of four different tablets to cure an illness. You would be crazy to take just three types of pill because you didn't like the look of one. At best you would dilute the cure and at worst you would nullify it completely.

If you do only 90 per cent of what a mentor advises, you may as well not bother at all. Be open to what they tell you, however tough it is to swallow, and do everything you can to follow their lead with full and unerring commitment. It will be to your benefit.

### Where to find the right mentor
I've already described how I turned to the written word when I first decided that I needed guidance from those who had been there and done it. Back then, I had no money for courses and didn't know who to ask for help, so the library seemed the logical place to start.

Today, of course, developments in technology have rewarded us with a wealth of information, and the internet in particular offers so many more opportunities for enlightenment. The wise words of motivational heroes (mine are Dale Carnegie, Tony Robbins and Deepak Chopra) are freely and widely available online, and there are literally millions of inspirational stories and videos from all over the world, all just waiting to give you guidance. Even today, if I ever get a spare half hour or so, I still surf YouTube, because I invariably come across a gem that really makes me think and spurs me on to do even better.

As I grew in confidence, following my long hours in the library, I summoned up the courage to ask business people I admired whether they would do me the honour of mentoring me. I would choose someone with skills in a discipline I believed I was lacking at that particular time – say, marketing – and get in touch with that person. I'd introduce myself and then say something like, 'I really respect you as someone who is outstanding in marketing. Could you possibly give me an hour of your time to guide me?'

I can honestly say, that every time I have asked, people have always responded positively, even when I was a million miles away from the position I am now in. I am convinced that most people, if they really believe the request comes from a genuine source who respects and appreciates their knowledge, will give up at least some of their time to mentor others. It is an incredible complement to be asked. And, from your point of view, the worst-case scenario is that you will receive a polite 'no'. Even if this does happen, you will have lost nothing but the price of a postage stamp or phone call.

Don't worry, either, about paying for a mentor. The most I have ever paid for all the help and advice I have been given over the years is the price of a lunch or dinner. None of my mentors have even broached the subject of payment. There *are* professional mentors, who charge for their services, but at this stage let's stick with those who simply agree to give up a few moments of their time to share their valuable perspective on your situation.

To get started, think of the smartest person you know – or have heard of – in your particular field, or the field you are looking to enter, and ask them to be your mentor. Finding out how to get in touch should not be an obstacle. You could begin by going back to the library (which is a great source of directories, trade magazines and general information that could push you in the right direction) or try the internet. Be *active* in your search. Buy the books of the person you are targeting and attend any talks they give. That way, when you turn up asking for help, that person will know you really do respect what they have to say.

Another potentially good source of mentors is teachers. As everyone knows (and as I mentioned earlier in this book), a good teacher can change your life. Such teachers care as much about their pupils as they do the curriculum and do everything in their power to give their charges the confidence to step out and follow their dreams. You may well have memories of a former teacher who helped and guided you in some way. Why not go back to them and ask whether they would be willing to help you once more, in your adult life? They would probably be thrilled to be asked – it would prove to them that their efforts had not gone unnoticed.

You may be lucky enough to know a successful businessperson or local leader, or even have a relative whom you admire. People who know you are more likely to say 'yes' and find some time to help you. All you have to do is ask.

Don't go for the soft option and ask a would-be mentor who isn't quite at the level you need but whom you're pretty certain will say 'yes'. In my experience, when you go for targets like these, you'll spend just as much time chasing them down as you would for a more ambitious choice, and in the end all you will get is second best. It is far better to believe in yourself, try for the best you can possibly get (or even beyond that) and enjoy the fruits of your success.

You may have to kiss a few frogs to find your perfect mentor, but it will be worth it. With a little help from a well-qualified friend, your transition from where you are today to the successful you that you have envisaged for your future will be smoother and faster than you ever expected.

## QUICK EXERCISE

### Surround yourself with the best mentors in the world!

Wouldn't it be amazing if your heroes from politics, business and sport could be assembled to personally mentor you in your quest for success? Imagine how powerful it would be to have your own boardroom filled with these greats, who would be able to advise you on your every move.

So, why not go ahead and put together this mastermind group?

This is not to suggest that you should begin a letter-writing and phone campaign to ask everyone from President Obama to the Dalai Lama to spare some time to help you out. However, why not use the power of your imagination to create your very own Round Table of power mentors?

It works – it really does. And this is how.

As this is all in your mind, you have the luxury of gathering whoever you like around you – whether they are dead or alive. You can also avail yourself of the services of a wide range of gurus from all types of disciplines, from spiritual leaders to inventors. So, first compile your list. You may choose former prime minister Margaret Thatcher, for example, for her strategic skills. Steve Jobs could be called in for his marketing and product-development expertise. Or, if advice on relationships is required, it might be prudent to call upon John Gray, the American author of *Men Are from Mars, Women Are from Venus*. The choice is yours, and you can line up as many or as few mastermind mentors as you wish.

Then, consider the questions about your situation that trouble you the most. In your mind, ask each mentor for his or her view.

You might ask your mentor something like: 'So and so has really undermined me and affected my attitude, what should I do?'

The spooky thing is, even though this is only happening in your head, your brain will automatically give a different view for each 'mentor'. For example, if the Dalai Lama is one of your famous mentors, he may be empathetic and sympathetic, while Lady Thatcher might give a firmer, more unyielding response.

All of this is, of course, your impression of what each person would say according to your perception of them, but that is by the by. What you will have done is take the time to stop and consider your situation in a number of different ways. In this way, you will probably come to a far more well-thought-through solution.

This exercise is a form of meditation in which you ask for guidance and inspiration. You will be amazed about how effective it is at clearing your head and helping you to find a way forward.

**Taking your transition map to the next stage**

This chapter has already given you a head start in the mentoring process, by providing you with exercises and tools to start shaping your future goals. In the following pages, we will go to the next stage in the transition process and flesh out some of the actions that will take you from your current state to your desired future state. This would also be a good stage at which to seek the additional input of a mentor. A one-to-one session with your chosen expert would be invaluable in validating what you have learned so far from this book and giving you helpful pointers on how you might add to your plan and personalise it to your specific needs.

Figure 6

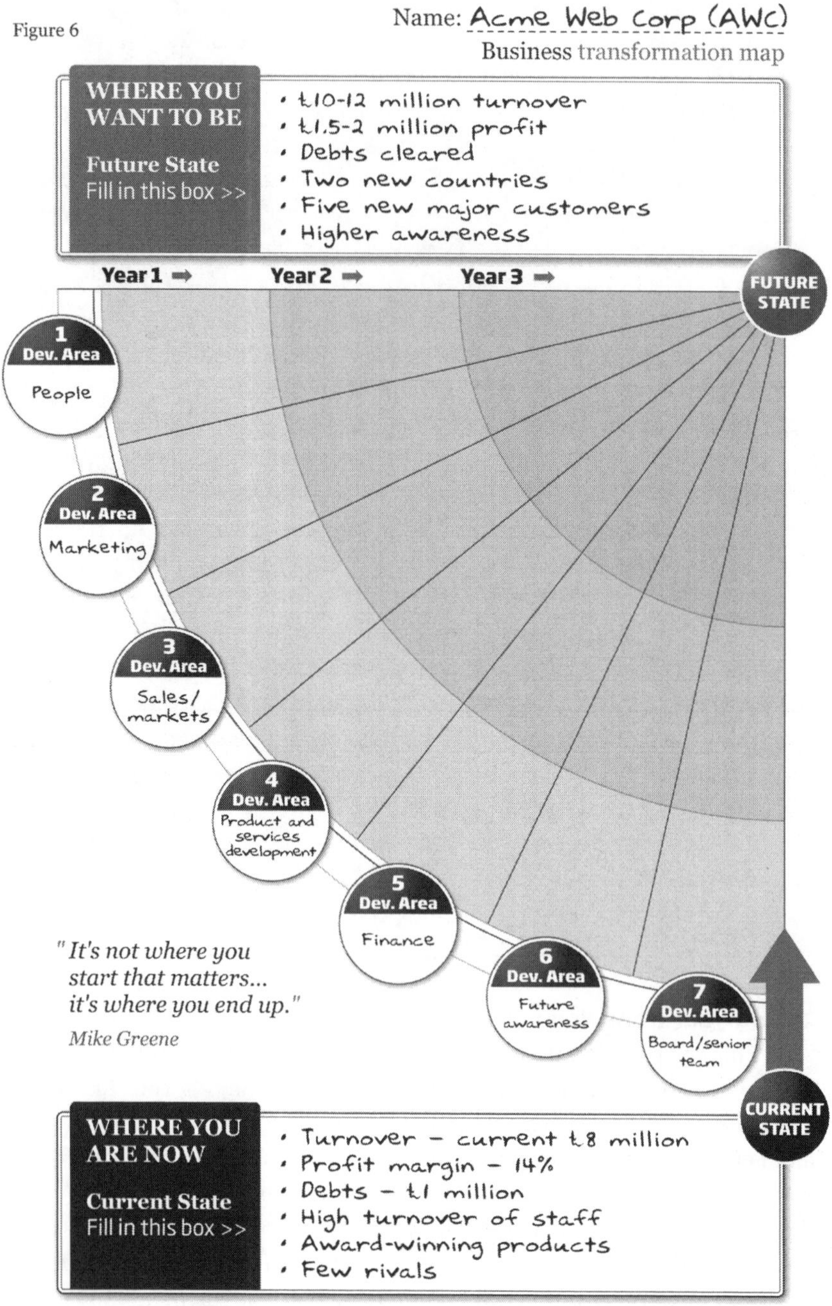

Name: Acme Web Corp (AWC)

Business transformation map

**WHERE YOU WANT TO BE**

**Future State**
Fill in this box >>

- £10-12 million turnover
- £1.5-2 million profit
- Debts cleared
- Two new countries
- Five new major customers
- Higher awareness

Year 1 ⇒    Year 2 ⇒    Year 3 ⇒    FUTURE STATE

**1** Dev. Area
People

**2** Dev. Area
Marketing

**3** Dev. Area
Sales/ markets

**4** Dev. Area
Product and services development

**5** Dev. Area
Finance

**6** Dev. Area
Future awareness

**7** Dev. Area
Board/senior team

CURRENT STATE

*"It's not where you start that matters... it's where you end up."*

Mike Greene

**WHERE YOU ARE NOW**

**Current State**
Fill in this box >>

- Turnover — current £8 million
- Profit margin — 14%
- Debts — £1 million
- High turnover of staff
- Award-winning products
- Few rivals

This next step in the progression of your transition involves breaking down the various areas that need change or improvement in order to reach your desired future state. To do this, you must analyse everything about your life, career or business that needs to be developed in order to make the huge leap to your goal.

In Figures 6 and 7, the transition plans for our imaginary business and personal cases have been taken to the next stage. However, to reiterate, the transition map process would work well for any type of transition, and there are other examples on my website: www.mikegreene.co.uk/tm. For the sake of continuity, though, we will continue with Acme Web Corp (AWC) and Joe.

Let's begin as before, by taking the mythical internet company AWC first. As you will recall, this moderately successful business plans to double its turnover within a three-year period, expand into new countries and greatly enlarge its areas of expertise.

In order to fulfil the massive growth curve it expects to achieve, AWC would need to look to all areas of its existing business operation. In particular, this would mean its staff, its marketing and its sales. At the same time, to plan ahead, the company would have to focus on new sectors and markets and on how to develop its new areas of expertise. It would also need to consider whether the senior team were ready and able to cope with the swift growth. These key areas of concern have been added to the transition map (Figure 6).

Each of the areas bisects individual years of the three-year plan, meaning actions can be plotted into each segment on a year-by-year basis.

In the case of Joe, who you will recall is aiming to triple his salary, clear his debts and sort out his personal life, there are a number of areas to be addressed. To increase his salary, Joe needs to look at his career and may have to consider adult education or retraining. Some sort of financial planning or restructuring is needed too, if he is to clear his huge credit-card debt and get on the housing ladder. In the case of his health and fitness, it is clearly time for Joe to address his diet and exercise regime. This might open up an opportunity for a new hobby in top-notch home cooking, but don't forget that Joe wants to change his relationship status too. He needs to get out more, so provision must be made for this on the map.

Figure 7 details the areas Joe must look at in order to reach his desired future state.

In the following section, we will look at ways to prioritise the actions that are needed. With so many parts of the plan to consider, though, once again it would be really useful to brainstorm this part with your mentor.

Your mentor may well have a different view from yours on the areas that

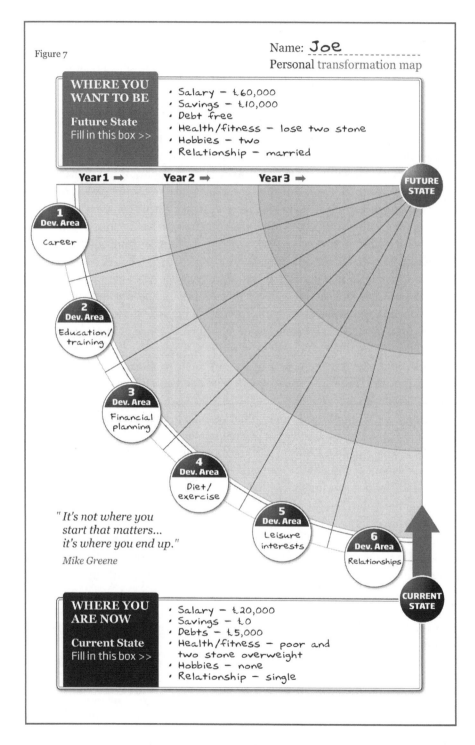

Figure 7

Name: Joe

Personal transformation map

**WHERE YOU WANT TO BE**

**Future State**
Fill in this box >>

- Salary — £60,000
- Savings — £10,000
- Debt free
- Health/fitness — lose two stone
- Hobbies — two
- Relationship — married

Year 1 ➡    Year 2 ➡    Year 3 ➡    FUTURE STATE

1 Dev. Area — Career

2 Dev. Area — Education/training

3 Dev. Area — Financial planning

4 Dev. Area — Diet/exercise

5 Dev. Area — Leisure interests

6 Dev. Area — Relationships

CURRENT STATE

*"It's not where you start that matters... it's where you end up."*
Mike Greene

**WHERE YOU ARE NOW**

**Current State**
Fill in this box >>

- Salary — £20,000
- Savings — £0
- Debts — £5,000
- Health/fitness — poor and two stone overweight
- Hobbies — none
- Relationship — single

most need enhancing or influencing in order to get to where you need to go. He or she might also disagree with you on which area it is most important to tackle first. That's fine – debate is healthy and it will get you thinking.

### Post-it note brainstorm

Although you will by now know the areas you need to tackle in order to get to your ideal future state, prioritising exactly what needs to be done and by when on your transition map can be daunting. After all, at this stage, there seems so much to do that it can be hard to know where to start. Indeed, before you write down firm actions that will lead you to your goals, the process can seem a bit fuzzy. Luckily, there is a great exercise to help you process all the potential actions so you can concentrate on the important steps now and leave some of the fluffier stuff until you're further down the line.

To get started, think in terms of the areas you have placed on your transition map and, together with your mentor, discuss actions that may improve them. Then, taking a book of Post-it notes and using one sheet per action, write down all the things you think you may need to do or learn to get from your current state to your desired future state.

Don't tie yourself in knots. This is not a business proposal for the bank; it is purely and simply a brain dump. It does not matter how raw or imperfect it is at this stage.

If you are considering a business transition, your notes may say things like:
- get better at delegation
- build a marketing campaign
- understand the opportunities in different sectors
- become a better presenter
- develop a motivating incentive scheme for the team
- research +/– with existing clients and find out why they like our competitors
- find out if we are up to date with technology and customer needs
- improve cash flow
- reduce debtors.

Or, if your transition is more personal, your notes may say things like:
- spend time with family
- lose weight
- meet someone special
- switch career
- retrain to fulfil lifelong ambition to be an artist.

Aim to produce about 20 Post-its. Think about everything you may need to do – and be ambitious. Then, draw up the chart shown in Figure 8 on a piece of A3 paper or white board in your office or home.

Place each of your Post-its somewhere on the scale, depending on how well defined the goal is. For example, 'losing weight' is a pretty fluffy goal until you give more details on how much you want to shed and by when. So, either put that Post-it firmly in the 'fluffy' quarter for now or do some work to make it a crisper goal. The more clarity you can add to goals, the more likely you are to be able to achieve what you want to achieve.

If you are working with a mentor for this exercise, you may like to discuss the merits (or crispness or fluffiness) of each note, moving them up and down the rankings accordingly.

Next, draw up the chart in Figure 9, which this time ranks goals on a scale between essential and trivial. This is a useful exercise. Very often in brain dumps people will say, 'I would love to do so and so' without having given the idea much thought. When they reflect on the idea more deeply, it sometimes becomes apparent that the goal, although worthy, will take quite a lot of effort without moving them much closer to their desired future state.

Looking at the scale in Figure 8, take each of your Post-its in turn and ask yourself whether that action will really help you to achieve your final destination. Once again, if any of the proposed actions seem a little vague when put under proper scrutiny, now is the perfect time to endeavour to crisp them up a bit – or 'crispify' them, as the renowned social scientist B.J. Fogg puts

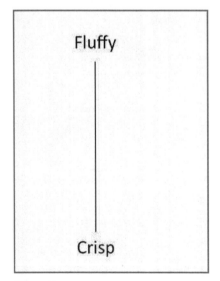

*Figure 8*

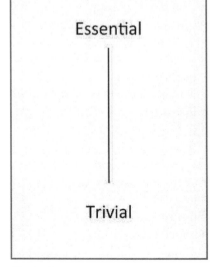

*Figure 9*

it during his Behaviour Design bootcamps.

For the third stage of this exercise, copy the chart in Figure 10. Using what you have learned from the previous two charts, move your Post-its over to the final chart, putting them into the most appropriate places on the grid. For example, say one of your goals is to improve your own marketability and that, through the crispification process, you have decided that to do this you needed to become a better presenter. Although it is now a firmer goal, if you've never done any public speaking before, it will still be pretty hard to do. So, put that note in the quarter between 'hard' and 'essential'.

Do the same for each of your Post-its. This exercise should give you a much clearer picture of what you are trying to achieve. Looking at your chart, you will see that the top-right quarter, between 'Essential' and 'Easy', highlights which are the low-hanging, easy-to-pick fruit that you could easy manage in the first year.

As you move diagonally away from this quarter, the goals will become harder and progressively less essential. However, they can and will get done. Anything that looks particularly hard can be put into year two of your plan – although it may seem tough now, in a year's time, when you've got yourself into gear, it will seem easy. Some of the hardest goals of all could even wait until year three, although, if you follow the transition map correctly, it is quite likely that what you can hardly believe is possible today will get done without problem sooner than you can imagine.

You will find it handy to go through this brainstorming exercise with your

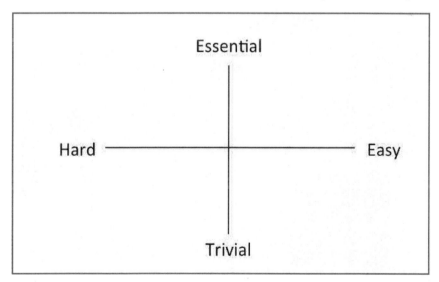

*Figure 10*

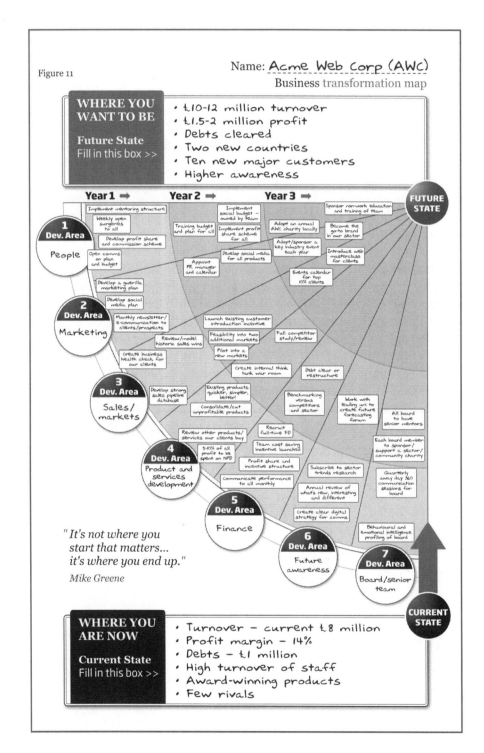

Figure 11

Name: Acme Web Corp (AWC)

Business transformation map

**WHERE YOU WANT TO BE**

**Future State**
Fill in this box >>

- £10-12 million turnover
- £1.5-2 million profit
- Debts cleared
- Two new countries
- Ten new major customers
- Higher awareness

Year 1 ➡    Year 2 ➡    Year 3 ➡    FUTURE STATE

**1 Dev. Area** — People

**2 Dev. Area** — Marketing

**3 Dev. Area** — Sales/ markets

**4 Dev. Area** — Product and services development

**5 Dev. Area** — Finance

**6 Dev. Area** — Future awareness

**7 Dev. Area** — Board/senior team

"It's not where you start that matters... it's where you end up."

Mike Greene

**WHERE YOU ARE NOW**

**Current State**
Fill in this box >>

- Turnover – current £8 million
- Profit margin – 14%
- Debts – £1 million
- High turnover of staff
- Award-winning products
- Few rivals

CURRENT STATE

chosen mentor, who will help you work through each goal, help you weigh up your abilities and spur you on to really stretch yourself.

After completing all the stages of the Post-it note brainstorm exercise, use what you have planned to add actions into the relevant years of your transition map. An example of how AWC's transition map might begin to shape up is shown in Figure 11.

In the route between the current and future states for the 'People' section, the bosses at AWC have decided to prioritise getting their staff on board with the company's steep growth curve. This will involve a complete change in the way they do business and a more open way of dealing with employees. Whereas in the past they may have played their cards close to their chest about management issues, they have decided that now is a good time to be more open about what they are trying to achieve. After all, with everyone pulling in the same direction, the company will have a far greater chance of fast growth. Putting in a mentoring structure for key personnel will also help at this stage. In year two, the management plans to introduce incentives and bonuses and may even bring in social activities for staff.

In terms of marketing, AWC has decided to kick off with some guerrilla marketing techniques –unconventional, yet low-cost, ways to get noticed and get people talking about the company. In addition, it will produce a monthly newsletter for those who are sufficiently stirred up by the profile-raising tactics to want to know more. In year two, as profits increase, this activity will be supplemented by a PR campaign and marketing activities targeting new sectors.

In year one, AWC plans to give its sales a boost by looking to the past and seeing what has worked well before. It also intends to put in robust health checks for all new clients, to make sure they are sufficiently lucrative.

Looking forward, AWC has pinpointed the sectors it would like to target in the future, as well as potential new areas to do business, such as digital. To back all of this up and maintain a constant flow of new ideas as the company grows, plans are in place for regular strategy retreats for senior and board-level personnel from year two.

Joe's transition map is, of course, very different. One possibility is shown in Figure 12.

Joe has decided to give his career new direction by asking for more responsibility at work and simultaneously beefing up his CV by signing up for management courses. Joe has long been interested in marketing and can see that it would be a valuable addition to his experience, so he has factored in a marketing course and is also investigating how he could do some more work by shadowing qualified marketeers. Financially, the first sensible op

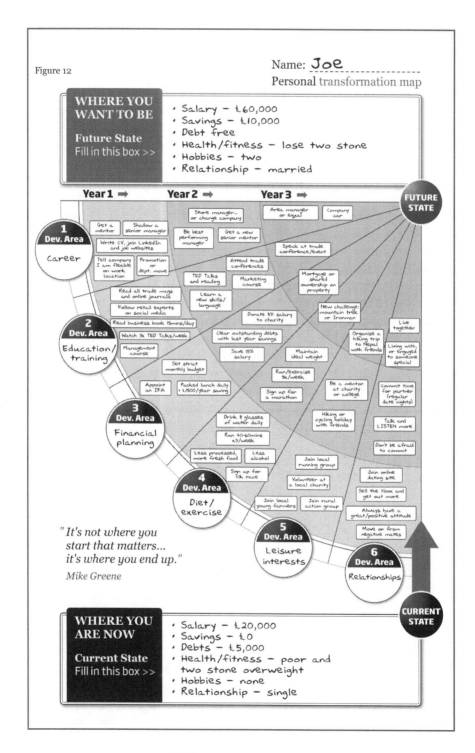

Figure 12

Name: **Joe**

Personal transformation map

**WHERE YOU WANT TO BE**

**Future State**
Fill in this box >>

- Salary — £60,000
- Savings — £10,000
- Debt free
- Health/fitness — lose two stone
- Hobbies — two
- Relationship — married

Year 1 ⇒    Year 2 ⇒    Year 3 ⇒    FUTURE STATE

**1 Dev. Area** Career

**2 Dev. Area** Education/training

**3 Dev. Area** Financial planning

**4 Dev. Area** Diet/exercise

**5 Dev. Area** Leisure interests

**6 Dev. Area** Relationships

*"It's not where you start that matters... it's where you end up."*

Mike Greene

CURRENT STATE

**WHERE YOU ARE NOW**

**Current State**
Fill in this box >>

- Salary — £20,000
- Savings — £0
- Debts — £5,000
- Health/fitness — poor and two stone overweight
- Hobbies — none
- Relationship — single

tion is to seek the advice of an independent financial advisor (IFA). While the IFA looks into what can be done to improve Joe's outlook, Joe will set himself a strict monthly budget.

To address the health and fitness side, Joe plans to adopt a sensible diet and begin running three times a week. He knows it will be a bit of an effort to begin with, but hopes to soon get into the rhythm and even be ready for a marathon in one year. However, running is a solitary pursuit, so Joe decides to sign up to a local running club to meet like-minded folk. He has also always been keen on environmental issues, so he plans to join a local group that is campaigning against a planning event that threatens a nearby area of outstanding natural beauty. Meanwhile, although Joe will now inevitably meet lots of people through his new activities, he factors in signing up to an online dating agency to be sure of broadening his chances of meeting the right woman.

These examples are just limited snapshots of the types of areas that Joe and AWC might target in their transition maps. They are purely for illustrative purposes, and many more actions would need to be added. However, these examples do give a fair idea of what needs to be done. Ideally, each section of your own map will contain up to half a dozen activities, all carefully thought through as a means to the desired end.

In the following chapter we will begin to look at how to make sure that all of these carefully-laid-out activities begin to get realised. It is, after all, important to stay focused on the end goal and to not to become distracted along the journey.

**Summary**
- The more you put in, the more you get out.
- Find good mentors.
- Learn from others' experiences (in person, through books and/or online).
- Use Post-it brainstorming to 'crispify' your priorities and establish time-scales for the transition map.

---

### QUICK EXERCISE

## Make hard goals easy with practice

When we are young, we are told that, if we want to succeed at sport or do well in exams, we need to practice. Then, somehow, over the

---

years we lose the habit. Imagine, though, how much better your chances of success would be if you took some time to practice once again. It would make the world of difference.

My drama teacher, Ben Meritt, once gave me some fabulous advice in this respect and I'd like to share it with you now, because it really does work.

Let's say one of your year-one goals is to get a better job. That's great. You're probably thinking of refining your CV, sorting out some sort of presentation and banging out a whole bunch of applications. That's great too. But why not go one step further? Why not start rehearsing for your interview? Apply for as many jobs as you can, from cleaner to fast-food waiter to checkout operator. It doesn't matter if you have no interest in the job whatsoever – the aim is to just get as many interviews under your belt as you can. You are about to embark on an intensive practice period towards interview success. You'd be amazed at what a difference it will make to your confidence when you finally get to the real thing.

A well-practiced interviewee can take over an interview, because the sad fact is that many interviewers are not that good at the job. In my experience, interviewers often end up simply talking about themselves when really they should be finding out more about the candidate in front of them. Then, once they run out of steam, they lapse into an awkward silence that inexperienced candidates are too nervous to fill.

After attending countless 'training' interviews, thanks to my drama teacher's advice, I learned how to break this awkward silence. I'd pipe up confidently, saying something like, 'would you like me to tell you about what I consider to be my best achievements and/or learning experiences?' Or, 'would you like me to tell you a bit more about the jobs I've had?' The poor interviewer was always both grateful and impressed. In the meantime, my confidence and marketability as a would-be candidate for any job I really did desire increased exponentially.

Look carefully at your list of goals. Is there an opportunity to practice any before you try the real thing? Practice really does make perfect.

## ADDITIONAL PPA EXERCISE

Depending upon your particular personality group – whether dominant, influencer, steadiness or compliance – you may either love or hate some of the exercises in this chapter. This section will give you some clues to understand how you are reacting to what you have read so far, in accordance with your personality type. It also gives some ideas on how you may best use this chapter for your own style of thinking and learning.

### Dominance messages
- Achieving big ambitions requires massive drive and energy.
- You can't do this alone.
- Find short cuts to your goal by learning from the successes and failures of others.
- Time spent on Post-it brainstorming will repay itself many times over.

### Influence messages
- Achieving notable success requires huge commitment.
- Seek out mentors who will bring out the best in you.
- Don't just learn from your personal networks; research other successful people too.
- Post-it brainstorming at the start will save time later on.

### Steadiness messages
- Constructing a secure future requires a big investment of time and effort at every stage.
- Don't hesitate to ask for support from successful people.
- Increase your chances of success by building on the experiences of others.
- Post-it brainstorming is key to creating a solid foundation for the transition process.

### Compliance messages
- Creating your ideal future requires investing 100 per cent of your inner resources.
- Choose the best in their field to be your mentors.
- Minimise risk by analysing the successes and failures of others.
- Use Post-it brainstorming to structure your thoughts at the outset.

## CHAPTER FOUR

# FOCUS ON THE RIGHT DIRECTION

Feel the fear and do it anyway – Susan Jeffers

Some years back, after many weeks of painstakingly teaching my youngest daughter, Amelia, how to ride her bicycle, we agreed that the time was right to venture further afield for her first big solo cycle. We selected a very rural country lane for the event, figuring that, aside from the two large ditches either side of the road, there was very little danger of any mishap, even if things did not go quite as planned.

Even today, some years after that outing, I still remember our joint sense of anticipation for this inaugural journey as we wheeled the bike up to our agreed starting point. We both recognised it for the important milestone that it was.

When the time came, Amelia peddled off confidently and, as I jogged beside her, I was filled with pride, as any parent would be. She'd remembered everything I had taught her and was riding with a good, steady style.

After a while, as she grew in confidence and even began to peddle slightly ahead of me. I felt secure enough to glance around a bit to take in the beautiful surroundings. A magnificent owl caught my eye as it soared above the hedge right beside me and I could not help but point it out.

Upon hearing my exclamation, Amelia looked around and, letting her gaze follow the direction of my pointing finger, she promptly cycled straight into one of the deep ditches that lined the edge of the lane.

'Why on earth did you do that?' I asked, as I picked her up and dusted her down, noticing that – thankfully – very little harm had been done.

'You told me to look over there and the bike just went that way,' she replied, as though this was the most obvious explanation in the world.

But, in a way, perhaps it was. When we embark on any new venture, we all start out moving purposefully towards our goal, focusing hard on the direction we believe will get us there. The problem is, as Amelia found the hard way, even in the first heady moments of tackling something new, sometimes we do allow ourselves to get distracted. Before we know it, we're focusing on entirely the wrong direction.

By this stage in the process, you will be setting out on your transition and will be preparing to start on the actions you have been carefully plotting on your map throughout the previous few chapters. This is the time where fear of failure and the reality of what you are about to do will really begin to sink in.

Remember that, although failures can be painful – particularly in the early days, when expectations are so high – they are also a great learning opportunity. For a start, they are an instant reminder, in terms that cannot be ignored, that you have strayed off track. Getting something wrong is the perfect moment to re-check your focus and make sure you are still heading in the right direction: towards the goals you have set out.

You will also find that there will be an endless supply of doubters and naysayers who will tell you something is just not possible or that you are already going in the wrong direction. Though it is largely alright to ignore these naysayers as long as your plans are sound, you may as well take advantage of their negativity to re-check that you are on course.

Going back to the taxi-driver analogy introduced in chapter one, you can't just assume that your ride will take you the way you wish to go. If you get into a conventional taxi and ask to be taken a certain route, very often the driver will insist he knows a better one. You may decide that he's right, but, if you don't agree, it is up to you to stand your ground. Your mental taxi driver may question whether or not it is possible to lose weight or start your own business, because perhaps you have tried before and failed. You have to push for what you want and insist in your mind that this time will be different. Make a mental note to regularly check that everything is going as you wish.

Don't panic when things do veer a little off course. It's not a disaster.

Getting something wrong is a lesson in itself and there are always positive things you can take away from mistakes that can inform, or correct, your future direction.

If I were Amelia's mentor instead of her concerned parent, I might have made the point that the ditch episode, although momentarily painful, taught her more than a week's worth of teetering around the garden. On that fateful day, she learned lessons about focus, steering and responding to outside stimuli far more quickly than she had by me standing beside her at home saying things like 'left a bit', 'right a bit', 'hold on tighter here' and 'off you go'.

A far more worrying scenario would have been Amelia being too worried that things might go wrong to have ever set off at all. If she had been older, this might have been the case: as we become more aware of what could go wrong and how painful the consequences could be, we become risk averse.

When setting out on any new venture or in planning to tackle new and ambitious goals, as you have now undertaken to do, fear of failure can be a real handicap. Fear is OK – even natural – but don't let it stop you doing whatever you want to do. If you do not keep your fear in check, it can paralyse you and stop you from focusing and doing the things you need to do to meet your ambitious transformation targets.

There is a perfect antidote to this reticence in the face of beginning something tough that I have often heard in America: 'set off and course-correct'. Bluntly, it means just get on with it! Don't waste time worrying about ditches, mishaps, falls or other obstacles because they may never happen. And, even if they do, it's no bad thing. Apart from anything else, there is very little point hesitating because it won't be until you get started that you will even find out what most of these obstacles are.

If you want to get from your current state to your desired future state, you must adopt a mindset in which you focus on where you want to be, regardless of the potential failures along the way. Better still, *encourage* failure by pushing the limits as hard as you can. Indeed, if someone in the initial stages of a transformation programme were to tell me that they had not yet had any mishaps, I would be seriously worried. It certainly would not be cause for congratulation, because lack of failure is one of the surest signs that things are not on track. It is a flashing alarm saying that you are not trying hard enough or that the goals you set were too easy!

In any ambitious programme, we all need a good mix of successes and failures, although obviously the successes should eventually outweigh the failures. Early failures are particularly useful because they allow you to learn about potential flaws in your plan, or where there are opportunities you may have missed. They may also show you that, although you meant to go to A, you were actually mistakenly heading doggedly towards B. They enable you make all the little adjustments you need and move forward with renewed strength and vigour.

I really believe each challenge and failure acts as another foundation layer that will help you secure and sustain your eventual success.

You can't allow yourself to be put off by hiccups along your journey, still less to give up altogether. Allow all your errors to impart a valuable lesson and then let them stiffen your resolve to keep trying and perfecting whatever it is you are learning to do.

If all else fails, remind yourself of your taxi driver. If you programme your mind to think everything is terrible and will end in disaster, that is exactly where your driver will take you. If, however, you take the opposite approach and see everything in life as positive, that is where you will end up. It is that simple. It is not that optimists have charmed lives and pessimists are doomed to fail every time. When push comes to shove, we all receive equal shares of triumphs, breakthroughs and knock backs as long as we put in the required amount of effort. It is simply down to how you view the world around you and how you instruct your taxi driver to act. Programme your mind to see the good things about your journey, even when it doesn't quite go as expected. If you think you can't achieve something, you probably won't; but, if you believe you can, anything is possible. And I mean *anything!*

### Forget the fall-back – focus on the upside

Thomas Edison, the influential American inventor and businessman, tested over 3000 filaments before he came up with his version of a practical commercial light bulb. In all the accolades about how this man literally lit up the world and transformed our homes and businesses, no one gives a second thought to the 3000 filaments that were discarded along the way. Edison did, though. Perhaps unsurprisingly, this clever and persistent man did not think of them as 3000 failures. When asked, he said he had simply found 3000 ways that his filament didn't work. More importantly, his experiments with those other filaments spawned a host of additional inventions along the way. Whenever his tests resulted in unexpected reactions, responses and occurrences, he was able to think laterally and put the 'failed' filament materials to good use elsewhere. Among his prolific inventions were the phonograph, the motion-picture camera, a battery for an electric car and a mechanical vote-recorder.

Edison's story proves that, when you are focused on the right direction and your brain is programmed for success, opportunity and optimism, you will find the right stuff pretty much wherever you look. Even when something does not initially appear to be what you are looking for, that's fine because it is more than likely that it will present a breakthrough in some small way, or will teach you a useful lesson.

Don't forget, either, that the transformation you are setting out to achieve here is extraordinary. You are not trying to change a few things in your life to make you feel a bit better off. You are aiming to dramatically improve every aspect of your life. Just as tweaking the design of the candle was never going to get Edison to the light bulb, you need to be thinking about revolution, not evolution. You are embarking on a change so significant that it needs a different approach. After all (to paraphrase Einstein), the height of insanity is to keep doing the same thing and expect different results.

Now you have set out your desired future state on your transition map, it should be clear to you that a little hard work won't be enough to see you through the journey. You need to focus and be prepared for a few knock backs and failures along the way.

One of the biggest mistakes you could make at this stage would be to try to cushion yourself against these failures. You know the sort of thing. You see someone going for something big and then adding the proviso, 'I can always go back to where I was if it doesn't work out.'

If you start to think in terms of there always being a fall-back position, it will stop you getting to where you want to be. For this revolution, you need to burn all your bridges and believe in what you are doing.

I came across a great example of how powerful this philosophy can be when I heard Fred W. Haise, one of the *Apollo 13* astronauts, speak at an event. Fred was talking about the famous space mission, which was originally intended to be a moon landing but was aborted after an oxygen tank on the rocket exploded and crippled the service module upon which the command module depended. What followed was a race against time, as experts on the ground and the astronauts on *Apollo 13* tried to figure out how to get the crew back to earth and keep them alive long enough to make the journey. The crew themselves had to do all of this while suffering the most extreme hardships caused by limited power, loss of cabin heat, a shortage of water and a build-up of carbon dioxide on board.

Haise described eloquently how the crisis caused an interesting anomaly. All of the training he and his fellow crew members (Jim Lovell and Jack Swigert) had undertaken was underlined by the mantra that failure was not an option in any aspect of their training or mission. Yet, here they were in a situation in which they had to reprogramme their brains to think in an entirely different way and focus on a new direction completely. If they didn't manage to turn things around successfully, they would all die. Haise said that, with no fall-back position or alternative 'easy' way out, the crew pretty quickly found a whole new way of thinking – and of course they had a very successful outcome, by surviving the fated mission. In a dramatic way, the *Apollo 13* story shows that burning one's bridges ensures a more single-minded, measured and intense response to setbacks.

The setbacks you will experience will not be anything like as severe as being stuck in space in an ailing rocket with no obvious means of escape. They are far more likely to be small problems caused by your own inexperi-

---

### QUICK EXERCISE

## Ask yourself: did you really fail?

How many times have you looked at an event in retrospect and admitted that, although it seemed disastrous at the time, it was actually one of the best things that ever happened to you?

Perhaps it was an unexpected redundancy that forced you to start that new business you'd always dreamed of. Or maybe it was the time when you were dumped by a long-term partner, opening the way for you to find the love of your life. Or perhaps you had to give up a sport because you couldn't ever make a team, so you tried a completely new one and found you had a real talent.

There is enormous power in failure, especially when we learn lessons from it. And, guess what, once you've used the opportunity and turned the situation around to your advantage, you will always be better off.

Take a piece of paper and write a list of events in your life that at the time you thought were a complete disaster. You know, the sort of occurrences that probably had you sitting down with your head in your hands in despair.

Now you have done that, write down beside each event what you believe you learned from it, or what unexpected opportunity or event opened up as a result of the setback. You'll be amazed at how positive all your failures turned out to be.

So, this begs the question, is there really anything you should be afraid of?

---

ence or lack of knowledge that simply require a small course-correction to get back on track.

Occasionally, setbacks will occur that are beyond your control, caused by some outside factor you hadn't bargained for and may not have even imagined was an issue. That shouldn't send you scuttling for the exit, though. You can't control everything so you simply need to accept that this will be part of the journey and be prepared for the unexpected.

### Don't change direction at the drop of a hat

For a moment, let's stick with the cycling analogy that opened the chapter and imagine ourselves peddling along, with great determination, in the early stages of our journey towards our future state. The counterparts of those who inadvertently lose focus and veer off in the wrong direction (thus learning an essential lesson) are those who run into a spot of bother, or see a potential danger ahead, and execute a dramatic left or right turn to avoid the hazard.

We all know people like this. At the first sign of a problem or hardship, they wobble and change their job, or end their relationship, or up sticks and move away.

They justify their abrupt about turn by saying something like, 'I have to leave because I'm not getting what I need' or 'They will never pay me what I want.'

They lose confidence and their knee-jerk reaction, which they firmly believe will solve their problems at a stroke and move them forward, is to change their geography and start again. Even if they have a residual doubt that this will actually make them any better off, they'll justify their decision to themselves by saying that they have been stagnating for far too long, watching others sailing by and going on to bigger and better things.

The flip side of this thinking is a rather daring technique pioneered by Formula One drivers on how to avoid severe crashes. An important part of the drivers' training routine is to drive straight towards the point of impact when they see a crash. At the speeds they travel at, this is the least likely place for anything to be happening by the time they get there. It takes some guts to do this, but, if drivers swerve in a bid to get out of trouble, the chances are they will actually plough straight into the worst possible place.

When people lose confidence, they tend to look about them and conjure up visions of how the outside world has failed them. In this blame game, the accusations come thick and fast. They'll say their employer has not been quick enough to recognise their talent and hard work. Or perhaps members of their family are too self-absorbed to give them the attention they crave. Or maybe their partner doesn't make enough effort. It may even be all three at the same time. So, they change their geography, by switching their job or relationship or hometown, in the belief that this will automatically give them the happiness they desire. Except – this will not work.

Changing direction and moving your geography will not guarantee you happiness or a fast track to your desired future state. It is a miscalculation. Why? Because it can't change you on the inside. If you take this path, you will simply be entering a cycle in which you will do the same thing again a few years later: change your geography and start again.

No, the only way to transform your situation is to carefully work out what you want and where you want to be, define the direction you have to take and keep at it. If you sit down and work out your current and desired states, as we have done in this book, you will find that you are far better off sticking to the plan. It will be tough, but, if you are prepared to take a few knocks and learn from your mistakes, you will get there in the end. Chopping and changing will simply stop you in your tracks.

If you are still doubtful, think about it logically. Let's take as an example a plan that has an ambitious salary target as one of its goals. Believe it or not, in the majority of cases, if you have a big salary rise in mind, you will be better off aiming for it in your current job. Changing job is not easy, and, while if you are successful you may see a small wage hike when you join a new firm, you are unlikely to move on a great deal for at least a year or two afterwards and will spend all that time treading water. Meanwhile, imagine what you could achieve at your old firm by impressing your boss with your ideas, energy and vigour!

Similarly, do you really need to discard your relationship because it no longer seems to have that spark? You may have years of marriage under your belt, but because you can't be bothered to put the effort in, decide you'll be better off walking away. But is that really the best thing for you? How long will it take you to find another secure and loving relationship? Indeed, will you ever find one that is as good as, or better than, the one you have now?

The simple truth is: if you take the direct route between your current and desired state, rather than veering off at a tangent every time things look a bit tough, you will get there a lot quicker.

If you do find yourself feeling that things are not going your way, or perhaps are taking longer than you had hoped, it is always prudent to pause for a moment and analyse your situation before haring off in another direction (there are ideas on how to do this effectively in chapter seven). In the majority of cases, you will find that the bulk of your frustration is down to the fact that things are not happening quickly enough, not because you have experienced failures per se. If you don't take the time for reflection, before you know it, you will have instructed your internal taxi driver to take you on a new path and will have fallen straight into the trap described here.

An alternative course of action is to liken your feeling of frustration to the one you get when you get caught in a traffic jam. You are always better off pulling over and getting a cup of coffee while the snarl-up is cleared than heading off on a new and uncertain route in the hope it will save you a few minutes. It seldom does and simply takes you further away from where you are trying to be.

When you get frustrated, use the feeling as a cue to pause for a few moments to reflect on the situation. Once you have taken time to breathe and examine things properly, you will find a new perspective that you may not have considered in your feelings of dissatisfaction. These lessons are an ongoing part of your journey and should be welcomed as such. Pressing the pause button makes far more sense than suddenly stopping everything to pursue a direction that is not in your best interests.

### Taking an imperfect direction

As you set out on the process and begin to face up to and even welcome your fears, your transition map should be in pretty good shape. Following the exercises in the previous chapter, you will have laid out some impressive targets along your journey towards your future state. Now you will begin putting your money where your mouth is, so to speak. As an aid to help you refine it still further (because you will be constantly refining your map through this journey), I would like to share with you some inspirational words from the Japanese psychologist Shoma Morita. Morita, who was strongly influenced by Zen Buddhism, believed that we all need to move forward a little at a time, even if we are not 100 per cent sure we will succeed. He believed that the world is not a perfect place, where all is rosy, but that once you accept this you will gain comfort from knowing that setbacks are a part of what happens to us all. He said:

> *Give up on yourself. Begin taking action now, while being neurotic or imperfect, or a procrastinator, or unhealthy or lazy or any other label by which you inaccurately describe yourself. Go ahead and be the best imperfect person you can be and get started on those things you want to accomplish before you die.*[4]

---

4. Shoma Morita, *Shinkeishitsu no hontai oyobi ryoho*. Originally published 1928.

Too many people hesitate, or wait until things are 'just perfect' or the circumstances are 'just right', before they begin a journey. But, as we all know, that day never really happens. We all get through our lives being that little bit imperfect. The important thing to ask yourself is: why not just get on with it? Or, as in the quote that opened this chapter, feel the fear and do it anyway.

Although we have been very specific to date in our target actions, it is time to revisit our Post-it brainstorm and see if we can introduce some more ambitious targets to go on the map. Be brave and dare to dream. The bolder you are, the more you will be able to speed up the journey towards your desired future state. Remember, as Morita says, it doesn't matter if you have (mistakenly) labelled yourself as imperfect; just go ahead and be the best imperfect person you can be.

A great way to define these additional goals is to think about what you definitely *don't* want. You may say:

*'I don't want poverty.'*

*or*

*'I don't want an unfulfilled relationship.'*

*or*

*'I don't want to be 18 stone in weight.'*

Once you know what you don't want, you can begin to focus on what you do want. If, for example, you no longer want to be 18 stone, what weight do you want to be? Twelve stone? OK, put it on your transition map.

As you become emboldened, think back to the dreams of the future that you had when you were a child of seven or eight years old. That was probably a time when you had great clarity about what you really wanted before it was drummed out of you by the education system or your parents or by people who had an entirely different agenda. Perhaps you wanted to sail around the world, or be a fireman or an artist. Remember these dreams and how they made you feel and think how they may fit into your transition map.

Now is a good time to revisit your transition map and look at your goals once again to check that your plans are really stretching you to your limits. Over the course of the previous few chapters, you will have set your future/desired state. What you need to do now, with the benefit of what we have discussed so far, is decide how confident you would be adding 30–50 per

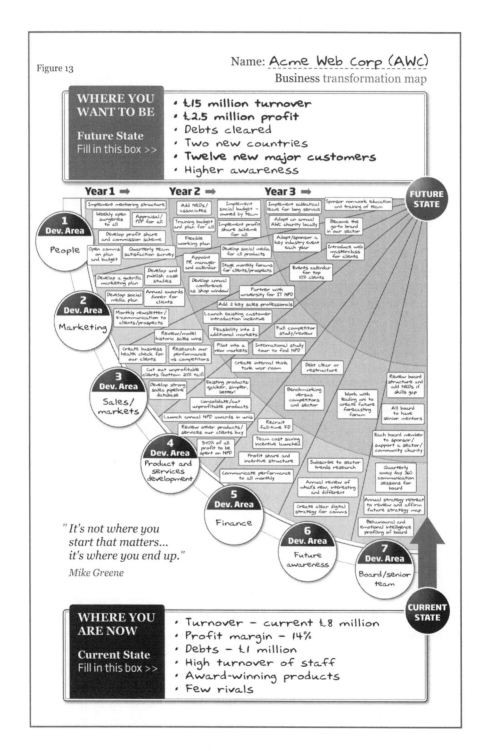

Figure 13

Name: Acme Web Corp (AWC)

Business transformation map

**WHERE YOU WANT TO BE**

**Future State**
Fill in this box >>

- £15 million turnover
- £2.5 million profit
- Debts cleared
- Two new countries
- Twelve new major customers
- Higher awareness

*" It's not where you start that matters... it's where you end up."*

Mike Greene

**WHERE YOU ARE NOW**

**Current State**
Fill in this box >>

- Turnover – current £8 million
- Profit margin – 14%
- Debts – £1 million
- High turnover of staff
- Award-winning products
- Few rivals

cent to the goals we set in chapter one.

Thus, in our fictitious example of Acme Web Corp (AWC), the directors are confident in their success so far and have agreed to ramp up the projected future state and the actions required to get the company there (shown in Figure 13). The new goals now incorporate a £15-million turnover (up from £10–12 million) and a profit of £2.5 million (up from £1.5–2 million). The company has also resolved to sign up a further two major new customers. To achieve this more ambitious target, AWC has adjusted its actions in years one, two and three to include initiatives such as a sales ambassador programme, behavioural profiling for staff to get the best possible performance from them, a digital media strategy and a feasibility review of new markets. There is a whole lot more to do, but, buoyed by the success of the transition so far, the directors now know it is possible.

Joe is similarly optimistic. Things have been going well for him since he adopted his plan. He has already achieved a promotion at work and the accompanying salary rise has gone a long way towards clearing his financial woes. On a personal level, he is preparing for his first marathon, has shed a stone and a half and has met a very nice lady called Louise at the local campaign group. He is, therefore, almost certain to meet his goals if he continues at the same rate of growth. It therefore makes perfect sense to extend those goals, so he continues to stretch himself. His new future-state ambitions are shown in Figure 14.

Go on, try it for yourself. Write down some stretched goals for your own plan. What do they look like? How do they make you feel? How much would adding to them change the actions in each year? What if you could achieve the heightened future state by making the actions even more crisp and focused?

If, after creating these new 'stretched' goals you are happy and motivated by them, redraw your map and adjust your plans/actions to deliver accordingly. By now, you should know it is possible.

Sometimes it really is just about thinking *bigger*.

Adjusting or stretching your goals by as little as 10 per cent will change the rate of your success exponentially. If you don't feel able to commit to this, that's fine. You are moving in the right direction anyhow. Maybe you could stick with your original plan and review it in a year, when hopefully you will be well on the way to your future state and your belief in what you can achieve will be stronger.

Drawing up a life plan and refining it as we have here should already be providing you with a source of great comfort. Visualising what you are going to do and how you will get there is a very motivating thing. Now you have the

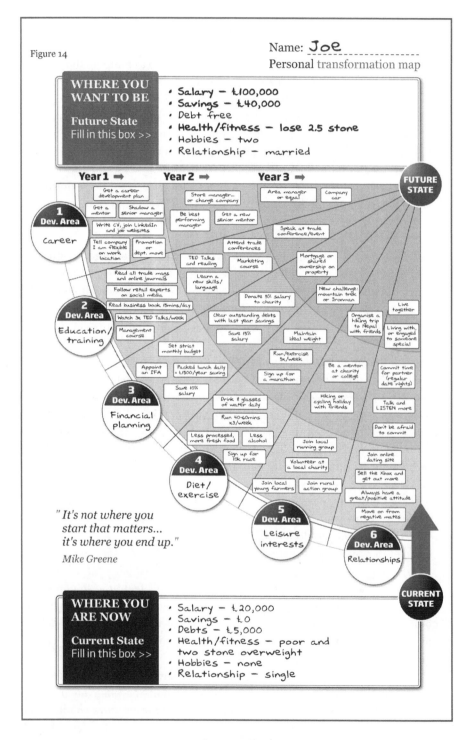

Figure 14

Name: Joe

Personal transformation map

**WHERE YOU WANT TO BE**

**Future State**
Fill in this box >>

- Salary — £100,000
- Savings — £40,000
- Debt free
- Health/fitness — lose 2.5 stone
- Hobbies — two
- Relationship — married

" It's not where you start that matters... it's where you end up."

Mike Greene

**WHERE YOU ARE NOW**

**Current State**
Fill in this box >>

- Salary — £20,000
- Savings — £0
- Debts — £5,000
- Health/fitness — poor and two stone overweight
- Hobbies — none
- Relationship — single

combination of a plan and motivation, not to mention a stubborn refusal to be bowed by fear, it is going to be tough to distract you from your goal. Now, that is pretty powerful indeed.

**Summary**
- Surround yourself with visual reminders of your desired end state.
- Keep moving towards that goal and don't get diverted or distracted from your plan.
- Embrace setbacks as an opportunity.
- Welcome your fears[5] and harness the adrenalin they generate.

## ADDITIONAL PPA EXERCISE

This section will give you some clues to understand how you are reacting to what you have read so far, in accordance with your personality type. It also gives some ideas on how you may best use this chapter for your own style of thinking and learning.

### Dominance messages
- Pin up the written description of your future state as a regular spur to action.
- Stay focused on that goal.
- Use setbacks to develop your experience and skills for the next challenge.
- Backing away is weakness; you are not weak, so grasp the nettle.

### Influence messages
- Pin up pictures of your ideal future; they will act as a constant motivator.
- Avoid enticing distractions, especially when the going gets tough.
- Every setback is an opportunity to grow yourself.
- You won't feel pride if you back off, so, whatever the outcome, face your fear head on.

---

5. Note that a Thomas International PPA report will provide more information about your basic fears. If you wish to complete a PPA, visit my website: www.mikegreene.co.uk/ppa.

### Steadiness messages

- Pin up your transition map as reassurance that you are moving in the right direction.
- Don't be tempted into making a detour.
- Recognise setbacks as temporary blips from which you can extract some learning.
- You were brave enough to start this process so gather your strength and bite the bullet.

### Compliance messages

- Pin up your transition map so that you can monitor your progress towards your goal.
- Don't get bogged down in the detail but keep moving forward.
- Use setbacks to expand your knowledge and develop new skills.
- The risk of doing nothing usually outweighs the risk of taking action, however scary.

## CHAPTER FIVE

# LITTLE THINGS MAKE ALL
# THE DIFFERENCE...

*Great works are performed not by strength but by perseverance*

*– Samuel Johnson*

Long, long ago, when the inventor of the game of chess showed his creation to the ruler of his country, he was asked to name his reward. The wise inventor considered this offer for a moment and then asked that a grain of wheat be placed on the first square of the chess board on the first day, followed by two on the second square the next day, four on the third square on the third day and so on, doubling the quantity of wheat grains on each square every day. The ruler accepted the offer without much thought, although he did feel a little perplexed as to why the courtier seemed to be asking such a low price. He ordered the treasurer of the kingdom to count out the grains of wheat and make sure they were given to the inventor. A week passed and still no wheat had been given out. The exasperated ruler sent for his treasurer and demanded to know the reason for the delay.

'It would take you more than all the assets of the kingdom to pay this reward,' said the embarrassed treasurer, who had been grappling with the exponential calculation all week. 'You owe 18,446,744,073,709,551,615 grains of wheat!'

It is astonishing how rapidly small beginnings can grow, as this legendary tale shows. As you can see in the table below, which shows doubling for just 30 days rather than the 64 days needed to fill a chessboard, while the early numbers are tiny, they quickly progress to an astonishingly large size.

One of the complaints I most often hear from people embarking upon a major transformation plan is, 'Whatever I do doesn't seem to make a jot of difference.' My retort is, *everything* you do makes a difference, even the smallest thing, and, as you can see from the table here, these small things all build up relentlessly towards achieving very big goals indeed. (The other more flippant remark I make in this circumstance is: if you're ever tempted to think little things don't have an impact, try sleeping in a room with a mosquito!)

Each stage we have tackled so far in this book is a small, yet very important, step towards your eventual goal. We've thought about the goals we want to achieve, we've focused on and dismissed our negative beliefs and we've sought out others with the necessary skills to be our mentors. Each part of this process should make you feel more confident and more able to do groundbreaking things. On their own, any of these things will be relatively small steps. But, taken together, in sequence they add up to some quite powerful progress indeed.

Imagine a modern-day equivalent of the wheat and chessboard story. Say, for example, an entrepreneur starts a new business venture with some fairly ambi-

| Day | Total |
|-----|-------|
| 1 | 1 |
| 2 | 2 |
| 3 | 4 |
| 4 | 8 |
| 5 | 16 |
| 6 | 32 |
| 7 | 64 |
| 8 | 128 |
| 9 | 256 |
| 10 | 512 |
| 11 | 1,024 |
| 12 | 2,048 |
| 13 | 4,096 |
| 14 | 8,192 |
| 15 | 16,384 |
| 16 | 32,768 |
| 17 | 65,535 |
| 18 | 131,072 |
| 19 | 262,144 |
| 20 | 524,288 |
| 21 | 1,048,576 |
| 22 | 2,097,152 |
| 23 | 4,194,304 |
| 24 | 8,388,608 |
| 25 | 16,777,216 |
| 26 | 33,554,432 |
| 27 | 67,108,864 |
| 28 | 134,217,728 |
| 29 | 268,435,456 |
| 30 | 536,870,912 |

tious targets for the future. He must prepare himself for the fact that, in the early days, he will hardly earn a thing. For illustrative purposes, let's change the days on the table to months and imagine this entrepreneur only takes home a pound to show for all his blood, sweat and tears in that first month. In month two, he may only manage to better that by a small amount and will have to scrape by on £2. Even if he manages to double that figure by month three, he will still only have £4 to show for his efforts. However, instead of looking at his progress in terms of what he is making now and how little he is earning while putting in so much effort, he could be looking at the situation in a more positive way. Thus, how would he feel if he knew that the fruits of his hard labour, which are doubling in value every month, could rise to a cool £8.3 million by the end of the second year of trading? That must be worth a few months' hardship.

What is more, working through each step, however incidental it may appear to the long-term goal, lays down some very necessary personal preparations for where you want to end up. Each day, each small step you take gives you the learning and experience you need to withstand the stringent plan you have set yourself and to enjoy your goals when you meet them.

If that entrepreneur who began on £1 in the first month had instead won the lottery and begun trading with a million or so in the bank, he wouldn't have been nearly as successful as if he had worked his way up from nowhere, gaining valuable experience one day at a time.

Once you start looking at your daily efforts in terms of how you will get a compound benefit further down the line, everything seems very different. It certainly helps in terms of withstanding the pain of perceived slow progress to remind yourself of what it will achieve in the months and years to come.

The reality is, you are unlikely to start your journey with millions in the bank. Apart from anything else, if you had that to fall back on, you probably wouldn't be embarking on this transformation. Once you understand, though, that the few grains of wheat you do start with can be made to multiply exponentially with hard work, you will see things in a very different light.

This philosophy can be applied to every area of your life and work because little things really do make all the difference. When I embarked on my own transformation plan some years ago, I became very worried that I was no longer able to spend as much time reading as I would have liked. As described above, I had got into the habit of reading biographies of great men and women I admired when I was in the early days of my bankruptcy. I had a thirst for knowledge and found reading books written by people I admired a great source of inspiration. The trouble was, as my business interests took off and I began to work long hours, I found it harder and harder to fit in time for reading.

I mentioned this to one of my early mentors and he had some very wise words. 'If you read for just 15 minutes a day, that equates to 90 hours over an entire year, which is enough to master most subjects thoroughly,' he said. 'Make some time because it will be worth it.'

Taking heed, I resolved that, however tired I was at the end of the day, I would set aside 15 minutes before I went to sleep to read my business books. This was not always easy, particularly when I was exhausted from the day's labours, but I made sure I found the time and know I have continued to benefit from all the amazing things these people have written down. The little bits I read each day added up to make a big difference. If you don't care to read, you could try the myriad inspirational videos on the internet. I would recommend Ted Talks (www.ted.com), which holds a great selection of 20-minute talks from some of the world's finest minds. Alternatively, surf YouTube for videos by some of your own business and/or lifestyle heroes. Some people even read out bite-sized versions of their books online, so you get the best of all worlds. Just give it some time and you'd be amazed what you will find and just how much you will learn.

### Challenge yourself every day – it's addictive!

Once you know what you are passionate about and what your definition is of the success you seek, every single step you take towards your goal will take you a little closer to it. Those steps may not be life changing every time; you may not even notice some improvements. But, believe me, things are happening.

During the filming of *Secret Millionaire*, there was one young lad at Time Stop, a hostel for homeless young people, who I hardly noticed at the time. His name is Dan and he barely featured in the TV programme, except for the final moments, when my true identity as a wealthy benefactor was revealed and Dan let out an expletive before being given a sharp cuff around the ear by the centre manager. I didn't think much of it at the time, other than as an amusing interlude that broke up the tension sparked off in the room by the unexpected revelation. However, it turned out that my visit and interest in this worthy project had had an impact. Dan was affected in a small way by being involved in the programme, albeit on the sidelines. It lit a little flame of ambition in him that perhaps he hadn't previously known he had.

In the weeks following the filming of the programme, Dan was inspired enough to sign up to a 12-week Prince's Trust Team course that in itself took a lot of commitment and determination from the position he was then in. While there, he rediscovered an earlier interest in beatboxing, which is basically the art of making musical sounds using one's mouth, lips, tongue and throat. He loved doing this and had a real talent for it too, so much so that other lads started asking him for help and advice. Dan was more than happy to help out and in doing this also discovered he had an aptitude for teaching and inspiring others.

Once he'd finished the Prince's Trust course, Dan decided to get involved with charity himself and took up with Beat This. Beat This works with communities to build confidence, self-esteem and skills to help people get into employment and connect with their communities. Many of the people they support are disengaged from mainstream society or education and may have special educational needs, disabilities or mental health issues, or display challenging behaviour. The kids supported by Beat This look up to Dan, which has given him a great sense of purpose and responsibility.[6] Lately, he has taken his message further still and has become a public speaker, taking his story of hope and inspiration to an ever-widening audience of underprivileged youngsters, helping them to help themselves. Last I heard, he was even trying to get a beatboxing group into his local cathedral, in a bid to unite generations through the mixing of ancient and modern culture. Step by step, this lad has created an inspirational new life for himself. Who knows what he will go on to do next? It couldn't have been easy and there were probably many times when he wondered why he was doing what he was doing, but he persevered and look what he has done.

It can be tough to keep yourself upbeat when a dozen doors have been slammed in your face and it seems like you haven't moved an inch forward in weeks. However, every little step you take in the right direction will make a massive difference. If you stay determined and on track, one day you will turn back and see that you are already a million miles from where you started and well on your way to your successful destination.

Sometimes, it does help to have an extra boost, even if deep down in your heart of hearts you know that you are getting there, albeit slowly. One of the ways to keep your motivation from flagging is to set yourself small daily challenges to overcome. Watch out, though – meeting and exceeding these challenges can be addictive!

I came across this method when I first started training for a marathon. It was one of those goals that I knew would really stretch me to my limits, which was why I decided to do it. I had done very little running indeed be-

---

6. See www.beatthis.org/daniel-rockall.

fore the moment when I decided I was going to do the marathon. However, as always, I enlisted the help of an expert to help me. In this case, I was fortunate enough to work with American ultra-athlete Stu Mittleman. Mittleman's credentials are pretty impressive: he has set eight national and international long-distance running records, including a world record for running 1000 miles.

Mittleman was full of good advice on how to breathe efficiently, using the whole of one's lung capacity in order to get enough vital oxygen to the muscles. He advised me on how best to place my feet on each step and how to hold my arms. He also recommended that, when the going was getting tough, I should chant to myself. The sort of thing I could say was, 'Every day in every way I am getting better and better. Every day in every way I am getting fitter and fitter.'

One of the most useful pieces of advice, though, was to start small and build up. But, and this is key, I had to keep on going further, or faster, every day. I couldn't allow myself to get to a point where I thought it was OK to stay at the same stage for a little while. So, I started with a quarter of a mile and went on to half and then three-quarters, and so on. Doing something like that is inspirational. When you push yourself, you reap so many benefits. Not only do you get ever closer to your final goal and feel glad that you are doing so but you also can't help but seek out new and more ambitious ways of challenging yourself.

When you realise you can romp past targets that a few months ago you'd never have thought possible, it builds your confidence and fulfils you in a way you could scarcely imagine. It is so much better than pouring yourself a stiff drink to give yourself a boost, or hearing your mum saying how wonderful you are. You know for a fact that you have achieved something that connects with the great person you really are inside.

### Have fun and reward yourself
One of the best ways to avoid burnout while you strive to consistently take more challenging goals is to introduce some fun into your routine. If it is not fun, or you are not enjoying yourself, you will eventually give up.

Thus, for example, when I am running on my cross trainer, I always plug in a film on my iPad. I know that, if I tried to do 45 minutes on this contraption without it, I would be bored witless and might even give up. With a movie, though, I could easily put in maximum effort while running for one and a half hours and hardly notice the time pass until the closing titles started rolling. I do the same in my corporate life, punctuating the days and weeks with enjoyable moments and events that make

## QUICK EXERCISE

## Take the lamppost challenge

As human beings, we are generally our own harshest critics, yet we are also our most empathetic sympathiser too. When the going gets really tough, there is often a little voice in our heads that says something like, 'Well, you did have a late night last night, why don't you take it easier for today?'

If you decide to push yourself a little harder each day, you must ensure your plan has some form of structure. Otherwise, it can be hard to quantify how far you've come, and therefore opens up a possibility of not really pushing harder at all as time goes on.

For this exercise, I will stick with the running analogy from the above challenge, but the idea could just as easily apply to any other aspect of your plan that needs to see day-to-day progress.

Imagine you are just starting to train for a marathon and have not exercised for years. Running any sort of distance at all will be a challenge. Ordinarily, you may decide to set off, see how you go and walk for a while if it all gets too much. Instead, in this exercise, set yourself a target to reach before you allow yourself the luxury of a walk. For example, you could say you have to run the distance between two lampposts before being allowed to walk the distance between the next two lampposts. Or, if you like a real challenge and live in a rural area, make a vow to keep running until ten cars have overtaken you, then walk until another ten have gone by, and so on. Sometimes you will have to keep running for a long time, while other stints may be mercifully brief.

This type of exercise can be applied to almost any target. If writing reports is part of your daily schedule, for example, you could aim to produce 100 extra words before you attended to other things. Or, if you are an entrepreneur who makes artisan bread, you could gradually increase the number of loaves made between breaks.

You will find the experience of steadily pushing yourself harder and harder more enjoyable if you set targets and then meet, or even exceed, them.

everything seem worthwhile. Thus, occasionally I will take a few hours out to go to the cinema with my wife, or I will ensure I leave work early enough to go to watch my daughter's hockey match, or get my brother round to have a family-wide pizza-making session.

The important thing is to recognise the good moments. A lot of the time, we are so bound up on other things – with what may happen here or there, what disaster might befall us if something doesn't pay off, or how someone might do us wrong in the future – that we forget to live in the present. Pause for a moment, though, and think about your life now. Right now. You are probably in quite a good place. Most probably, you are curled up reading this book and will have ambitious plans for the future down on paper or perhaps even in their early days of action. Yes, there are a few hurdles to overcome, but, if you ignore them for just a second, things right now, at this moment, are not that bad.

Believe it or not, you started out life living for the moment just like this. All babies live for the moment. Give them some food, a cuddle and a warm place to sleep and they will want nothing more. As we grow older, we gradually become more aware of time and start looking to the future. By the age of four or five, kids start asking their families what they'll be doing today. A few years later, questions emerge along the lines of 'how many sleeps till Christmas?' When we reach our teenage years, there are worries about exams, college places and what jobs there will be after graduation. Then, these worries are superseded by concerns over money, mortgages and pensions. Ironically, it is not until old age that most people start looking backwards and seeking more enjoyment and fulfilment.

This may seem the natural order of things, but what is wrong with trying to live for now and enjoy what we achieve every day? The more you train yourself to live for the moment, the more you will enjoy it. You will recognise, understand and appreciate the small steps you make each day towards your goal and will start to feel pretty good about them too. If you are too busy looking at the far horizon – towards where you are going – you won't see what is special about what you have done today. The little things you do always make a difference.

I am also a great believer in rewarding myself for reaching milestones along the way. This was a lesson drummed into me by one of my early mentors. This fellow made his money by buying companies, breaking them up and selling them on at a profit. He was rather like Richard Gere's corporate raider character in the romantic comedy *Pretty Woman,* though not as charming or good looking (but I think that helped him because no one ever saw him coming).

## QUICK EXERCISE

## Scrapbook challenge

One of my early mentors said to me that a goal is a dream with a date on it, and he couldn't have been more right. This got me thinking about how I could get more clarity over my long list of goals, and I decided what I needed was to find an inspirational way to give myself a daily visible reminder of what I was aiming for. I happened upon a simple technique that really helped me to stay constantly focused on the right direction. It could do the same for you, too.

For this exercise, I would like you to imagine how you will reward yourself when you finally arrive at your future state as mapped out in your transition plan. What is your vision of the trappings of this success? Will you, for example, want to have a house with a swimming pool, a fast car, a holiday in the sun, or even a super-sleek yacht? Or, will it be all of the above and more?

Cut out pictures from magazines and brochures of the sorts of things you are thinking about right now. Don't worry about how far you feel you are away from attaining them at this moment – concentrate on the visualisation. Right now, the world is your oyster.

Find somewhere where you can paste these pictures so they are a daily reminder of your dreams. I stuck mine in my appointments diary, with a few pictures on each page. If you are not someone who uses a paper diary, you could paste them into your day-to-day notebook or perhaps put a few pictures on the sun visor of your car. Alternatively, you may like to find a way to scan them into your electronic diary, so when you call up a date you will be confronted by a picture of your dream house, or car, or whatever bonus it may be. Another option is to make a mood board of pictures that you can place on the wall near your desk. Or use the online mood board service Pinterest.com. What is most important is that you come into contact with these visions regularly but that they don't become like wallpaper, which you can easily ignore.

The reason you are doing this is to give your dreams clarity. We all find ourselves talking about the things we would like if we were better off, or daydreaming about how we would spend our money, but these thoughts flit in and out of our heads and can often get forgotten or lost in the business of everyday life. However, setting up visual reminders is a fantastic way to motivate you because it clarifies these goals and helps you see what your life will be like in the future. Chancing upon one of these pictures every day will help to keep your eye on the ball and will go a long way in preventing you from becoming disheartened when things don't always seem to go to plan.

You could firm up your dream-board by marking some aspirations on your transition map, adding in pictures of your rewards on the dates you will award yourself them, should you reach your targets. You may also like to hang on to your diary or notebook so that, when you attain a piece of your dream, you can rip out the relevant picture to show you have achieved it.

If you are still not convinced, or even think it is arrogant to give yourself lavish rewards for a job well done, think about it in another way. There will be a lot of pain on this journey, if you are really pushing yourself as hard as you should. What would be more inspiring to you: thinking about the pain ahead or the pleasure that will come from the future reward? The pain is something that will push you away and may even tempt you to give up, whereas the pleasure is something that will pull you forward.

This fellow worked very hard, but not all – indeed only a minority – of his break-up attempts came to anything. He was in a firm pattern of fail, fail, fail, fail and succeed. It could be months, even years, before something came good through, and in all that time he would shed a lot of blood, sweat and tears. Then, one day, it would all come good and he would make £2 million in a couple of hours. I really admired him because he had this insane ability to take failure. He was totally calm about trying and failing repeatedly because he knew he was in a numbers game and eventually something would come good.

So, I asked him his secret.

'You need to reward yourself on the way up,' he said. 'When I get a big payout, I always buy myself a treat.'

His idea of a treat was mainly what would be classified as boy toys – fast cars, a yacht, some gadget or other – but that is what he liked. Me, I have always liked watches, so whenever I reached milestones in my business or personal life I would reward myself with a nice watch. That way, whenever I glance at my wrist it reminds me of the event it took to get the watch. One watch, for example, was bought when I sold the first tranche of my consultancy him!, and whenever I pick it up it gives me a warm feeling. It also reminds me of the effort that went into getting to that stage, including the occasion in the early days of him! when I had to remortgage my house at a time when I could scarcely afford to, in order to invest in my fledgling business.

Obviously, the reward needs to be in proportion to the achievement in question. If you start from nothing and land a job, then go out for a meal or buy yourself a new outfit. If you land a massive contract, then you may like to buy yourself something more significant. Don't over-reward yourself because this sort of behaviour can only end badly.

My pet hate is when I hear people saying they have reached some amazing point in their life, after years of hard work, and that it was a 'bit of an anticlimax'. They were utterly in control of how to celebrate their own big-bang moment and the fact that it was an anticlimax can only be down to their own apathy.

You do deserve a reward when you reach milestones and the most important person to reward you is you, yourself. We all crave recognition, from the moment we are born. Self-congratulation is an important part of this. So, plan ahead and decide in advance how you will reward yourself when you make progress on your transition map.

### Who is in control? You are

On days when you feel that you are banging your head against a brick wall and getting nowhere, remind yourself that you are in control of your own destiny. You can decide how you will view what you are doing, how it has gone so far and where you may need to put some effort in next.

In his bestselling book *The Seven Habits of Highly Effective People*,[7] Stephen Covey talks about the space that exists between a stimulus and a response. That space is like a giant pause button and represents our power to choose. We don't have to react negatively to everything around us; we can pause, reflect and choose our response.

If, at first glance, things don't seem to be progressing as you would like, take a moment to reflect on the fuller picture before throwing your hands up in despair and declaring that what you are doing 'isn't working'. It is your call. How you feel about things is your choice.

Some years ago, I had to go into hospital for a procedure. The doctor warned me that, because of the anaesthetic they would be giving me, I mustn't drive for at least 24 hours afterwards. He also said I should not

---

7. Stephen Covey, *The Seven Habits of Highly Effective People*. Simon and Schuster, 1989.

sign any important documents during this period. As it happened, I had a meeting scheduled in London the following morning in which I would be required to sign some crucial contracts. After a moment's reflection, I opted to go through the procedure without anaesthetic. I had done a lot of meditation in the past and firmly believed that it would be enough to get me through the operation. The doctor, who was extremely doubtful about my choice, even to the extent of putting a drip into my arm in case I changed my mind midway through the op, said I was the first person to do it in this way.

As it turned out, I didn't need that drip at all. I meditated throughout the procedure and got through it just fine. I was in perfect control. I knew in my heart of hearts that any discomfort from this procedure was just that. When we feel pain, it is in our minds, following a signal from the body's receptors around the site of the wound, to our brains. I wouldn't opt for open-heart surgery in this manner, but I was glad that I proved to myself the power of my own mind.

We all have the opportunity to control our own mind and to open it up to recognise the little wins that make us stronger and stronger every day. The little things we do really do make all the difference.

---

### QUICK EXERCISE

## What was good about your day today?

'How was your day today?' It's a common, even banal, question that nine times out of ten we dismiss without giving it much thought. We're usually far too busy moaning about all the bad things that have happened.

However, taking time to reflect on the good things that have happened to you since you woke up this morning can have a significantly positive emotional effect.

Change the question to 'What was good about your day?'

Get into the habit of writing down at the end of each day, or telling a loved one, three things that were good about your day. Set a reminder alarm on your phone so you don't forget to do it.

You will be amazed what a boost it will give you when you consistently look at your world in this way.

---

**Summary**
- Each small step forward increases your knowledge and experience.
- The cumulative effect of small steps in the right direction is exponential.
- Set yourself increasingly demanding challenges along the way.
- Build in pleasure and reward yourself for reaching milestones.

## ADDITIONAL PPA EXERCISE

This section will give you some clues to understand how you are reacting to what you have read so far, in accordance with your personality type. It also gives some ideas on how you may best use this chapter for your own style of thinking and learning.

**Dominance messages**
- When progress seems slow, check your improvement against your transition map.
- Set demanding challenges to re-energise yourself.
- Make sure some activities are pleasurable for you.
- Decide what your reward(s) will be for reaching milestones.

**Influence messages**
- When progress seems slow, review your personal development.
- Set exciting challenges to motivate yourself.
- Have some fun.
- Decide what your reward(s) will be for reaching milestones.

**Steadiness messages**
- Be reassured by slow but steady progress towards your goal.
- Push yourself out of your comfort zone by setting tough challenges.
- Build in some pleasurable activities to provide balance.
- Decide what your reward(s) will be for reaching milestones.

**Compliance messages**
- Monitor the direction of travel rather than the size and speed of steps forward.
- Set stretching challenges to raise your game.
- Don't focus exclusively on serious matters; you need some pleasure too.
- Decide what your reward(s) will be for reaching milestones.

CHAPTER SIX

# ...BUT DON'T CONFUSE ACTIVITY WITH ACCOMPLISHMENT

One reason why so few recognise opportunity is because it is disguised

as hard work – Thomas Edison (attrib.)

Ryan is a very loud person who is always the life and soul of the party. He looks a bit like Buster Bloodvessel, the front man of eighties' band Bad Manners, who was famous for his bald head, rotund figure and even bigger personality. Bloodvessel's similarly larger-than-life doppelganger, Ryan, runs a medium-sized media firm and he drives his team to distraction.

If you asked the people who worked with Ryan what the problem was, they'd probably say something like, 'He never takes things seriously. His idea of a good day is disappearing for lunch at midday and coming back loud and drunk in the afternoon, disrupting the whole office.'

People from almost any walk of life would, quite understandably, struggle with this type of behaviour from one of their senior colleagues. They wouldn't be able to understand how someone who is in charge of an organisation is able to behave in such an apparently flippant way. After all, if someone doesn't look in the slightest way busy, how could they possibly be getting anything done? That is certainly how it seems to Ryan's colleagues.

Now let me share another side of Ryan's life with you. Let's accompany Ryan on a trip abroad, where he will be attending an industry conference.

On the way over, Ryan turns to the colleague accompanying him and says, 'We are here for five days and I have two objectives: I want to get Company A and Company B signed up and on our books as new clients. I know they are massive Blue Chip organisations, but I also know we can get them on board.'

And that is exactly what he does. True to form, Ryan doesn't attend all of the official talks and events that are scheduled throughout the conference. In fact, most of the time he can be found in restaurants and bars doing what he does best: being the life and soul of the party. But, he does what he set out to do and comes back with the two new clients signed, sealed and delivered, adding more than £200,000 of billings to his agency's books.

Although Ryan's methods are unconventional and drive his colleagues mad, he gets things done. He doesn't waste time on appearances, or on doing things that will not achieve his overall goal, which is to double the size of his business in the next three years.

If Ryan had been locked into an office and told he must settle down and get on with X, Y and Z, or in other words 'look busy', he would never have achieved half the things he has done. He would certainly not have won two £100,000-plus accounts over a few days.

Ryan may be unconventional, and his way of doing business may not be to everyone's taste, but to me he is the embodiment of what can be done if you focus on the goal and don't allow yourself to be distracted by having to *appear* active.

Far too many people believe that keeping busy is all they have to do to succeed in life. It isn't, which is why in this chapter we need to look at the relationship between activity and accomplishment.

In chapter five we explored how little things make all the difference. The other side of the coin is those who work their socks off day in, day out and yet don't seem to get anywhere.

'I don't understand it,' you'll hear people like this say. 'I'm working 24-7 and haven't had a day off in months, but I feel like I am going backwards.'

To an outsider, the answer is pretty obvious: if you are working that hard and not getting anywhere, you are clearly not doing the right thing! If people who feel this way only came up for air for a moment and looked around them, they'd immediately see that they were heading in the wrong direction entirely.

It is a huge mistake to confuse activity with accomplishment. There is a big difference between hard work and honest-to-goodness getting stuff done.

A great deal of the problem comes down to the fact that we've all been conditioned to believe that success always comes with hard work. Therefore, the train of thought develops that the harder we work the more successful we will become. Well, that is the case to a certain extent, but the truth obviously goes further than that. The world is full of broke experts who have worked their little socks off and have nothing whatsoever to show for it. Qualifications and ability are no guarantees of success.

A scattergun approach to goals never works. With a scattergun, there is so much blast going everywhere that, even if you do manage by some fluke to hit your target, you will hit it so gently that there will be virtually no impact. If you want to transform your life and reach your goals, you have to take aim at the target and remain focused at all times.

None of this is to say you shouldn't work hard; after all, as I said in chapter two, the only place success comes before work is the dictionary. However, you should think very carefully about what it is that you are doing that is keeping you so busy. Is it really taking you any closer to your goals?

By this stage in your transition, you will already have laid out some very clear goals and defined the activities you must undertake to get you there. Part of the reason that I emphasised earlier that you should be very clear about your aims and what they will mean to you is so that you avoid the activity/accomplishment trap.

As I suggested in chapter one, there is little point saying 'I want to be a millionaire' without articulating what it would mean to you, and hopefully by this stage you will have been very specific about your goals on your transition map. Perhaps this wealth might mean you'd be able to take the whole summer off with your family, or buy your parents a house, or be a full-time mum or dad, or simply spend an hour a day of 'me time' with a paper and a cup of coffee.

If you have clearly and concisely instructed your personal taxi driver to take you to your goal, the driver will by now have set off in dogged pursuit of that goal. Your taxi driver will not allow you to become distracted or diverted because the sat nav is programmed to take the quickest route possible to your goal.

If you were not absolutely specific in your goals, this is when the cracks will begin to show. Other activities will creep in and take precedence over your aspirations. Then, without a tangible outcome, you will find yourself trying to measure your worth and progress by the sheer number and breadth of tasks you complete. These superfluous activities will mount up and up, sending you spinning off course from your planned future state. As you grapple with all these extra things, while still trying to stay on track, you will simply end up tired, stressed and frustrated. It may even stop you from ever reaching your goal altogether.

Even if you follow your plan to the letter and have set some very specific goals, it will still be tough. There is no denying it. But, if you know where you want to be and celebrate each milestone on your journey, soon you will barely notice the pain you endured along the way. Better still, the hard work will all be concentrated on the correct outcome.

## QUICK EXERCISE

### Too busy? Sleep on it.

If you get that sinking feeling that you may have fallen into the busyness trap, where you are doing an inordinate amount of work for what appears to be no gain at all, press the pause button and review your situation.

Take time out for some cool reflection on where you are and what you are doing and think about it in the context of the bigger picture. Is any of this activity actually helping you to reach your goal?

A good technique is to do this just before you turn in at night. Say to yourself: I have this problem and I don't know what the answer is. Then, ask your brain to give you the answer in your sleep. Be careful to focus on the solution, though, rather than just the problem, or you won't sleep for worrying.

This technique is not as daft as it may at first sound. As I pointed out in chapter two, the brain deals with 100 million bits of information a second yet only allows a handful into your conscious awareness. If you can focus on solving the problem while you sleep, there is a very good chance that the process of pointing your mind in the direction of something specific will cause something to happen.

The chances are, when you wake up in the morning, you will be better equipped to refocus on your plan and stop doing the things that distract you and take you off course.

**Taking control**

If you ignore the bits you don't need to do, there is always enough time to meet your goals, however onerous they may be. Why? Because, if push comes to shove, you can always find a way.

I am reminded here of an acquaintance of mine who is a hugely successful and supremely focused businessman. When we first met, he owned the franchises for five coffee shops as well as several pharmacies, a couple of online stores and a whole host of other small businesses besides. He was, not surprisingly, crazy busy all the time. He literally worked every waking moment and always had his mobile phone glued to his ear, even when he was carrying on a conversation with someone standing in front of him. Then, suddenly, he contracted a virus that attacked his heart and within days he was left almost totally disabled. The doctors advised his wife to take away his mobile phone because the stress of a single call could spell his end, even though he was only weeks away from his 40th birthday. The medics had to pump drugs directly into his heart just to keep him alive and he was told he urgently needed a heart transplant because without one he would have only weeks left to live.

Luckily, thanks to the ingenuity of the medical profession, my friend got a new heart and is well on the way to making a full recovery, albeit on a lifetime regime of drugs to help his new heart. I spoke with him to ask whether he was going back to his busy commercial life. But, guess what? He will not be working 24-7 any more. From a position in which he honestly believed he could not spare even a minute a day, he suddenly found he could when he had to. His health scare forced him to re-evaluate his life and make sure he only did the important things. What is most interesting is his realisation that his businesses can still run without him being in control of every detail. In fact, as he discovered for himself, the measure of a great leader is how well their business runs when they are not there all the time!

If we really want or have to, it's amazing how it is possible to find the time to do the things that we really need to do. To do this effectively, though, you must be utterly clear about your goals and where you need to be.

Sometimes, achieving this is as simple as taking control of all the unnecessary things that you do in your day. It drives me mad when people I'm mentoring say they haven't done this or that because they ran out of time. Then, in the next sentence, they'll be asking me whether I managed to catch that amazing new series on BBC1. They just don't seem to get it.

They might say they get caught up in domestic chores. 'Hire a cleaner,' I say. 'Don't tell me you can't afford it. If your goals are that important, you'll find the cash.' Or, they might say they had to go grocery shopping, not for one moment considering that they could do it online in the evening and save themselves hours a week.

We all have various areas of our lives we can adjust to find more time to achieve the things we really need to do. All we need to do is take more control. Decide what is important and stick to it. Forget the rest of the stuff. It is just a distraction.

## QUICK EXERCISE

### Knowledge is power

There is no major project or process that I have been through without setting a goal first. Once I have set that goal, I go on to find out all I can about the task in hand by either reading about it or actively meeting with people who have done similar things.

Knowledge is part of your solution because, once you know some of the potential pitfalls or short cuts, you'll be well on your way. There are very few things in this world that haven't been done before, and thankfully many people have been kind enough to share their experiences in books or online. These people have laid down a super-highway of information for you and you'd be daft not to take a look.

Research like this will help your taxi driver because, once you start focusing on finding out more, your subconscious mind will begin to seek out everything connected with your goal and bring these things to your attention. It will help your taxi driver to discount all the silly, superfluous routes that distract you from your goal, thereby keeping you on the most direct route. This is rather like when you decide on the model of car you'd like to buy and then see them everywhere you go. Once you are completely tuned in to your ultimate goal and know everything you can about it, everything you do will bring you closer to it.

I will, however, add a note of caution to this section. Although I recommend that you find out about the task ahead, don't start your journey by throwing yourself into an intensive and lengthy period of research – this will distract you and even delay the beginning of your transition. There is always a danger that, when you over-research something, you will 'discover' enough pitfalls to give yourself an excuse not to do it after all. Knowledge is good, but don't overdo it.

One question you do need to ask yourself at this stage is this: are you being a busy fool? If you're being really honest, you might find that you're filling your days with the easier (albeit time consuming) stuff because it is less daunting than the rest of the things you need to do. Are you deliberately allowing yourself to get overwhelmed by unnecessary things? You may be giving yourself the illusion that you are in control and getting things done while blaming external influences for not achieving absolutely everything, but in your heart of hearts you know you aren't really any closer to your goals. And you are not.

This journey is tough, but take a deep breath and concentrate on being effective and getting the right things done. Once you do this, you'll be amazed about how much better you will feel about it all.

### Get others to support you

At this stage you may be thinking: hang on a minute, I've set specific targets and I'm sticking to my transition plan like glue, but the goals *are* pretty ambitious. Even if I wasn't getting distracted elsewhere, I'd be pretty hard pushed to get through everything I need to get done every day. There is just too much to do.

What about getting help? Sometimes, no matter how hard you try, you can't do everything by yourself, and a lot of the time it doesn't make any sense to even attempt to do so. If you are in a business situation and have people working for you, you must learn to delegate effectively. If your goals are more personal, there may be more willing helpers around you than you think. Sometimes you just have to ask.

When we worked on the transition map in chapter three, I mentioned how important it was to get the support of those around you. This means finding a more open way of dealing with colleagues and those close to you. After all, if people don't know what you are trying to do, how can they be of any assistance? Plus, if a number of people all pull together in the same direction, it will multiply the chances of reaching the destination in the time that's been set out. This is true whether you are trying to turn your life around on a personal basis or you are aiming to build up and sell a business.

Now, in our personal transition map example, Joe begins the process as a single man, but imagine that he was married with two young children. One of his early goals was to lose two stone in weight in order to significantly improve his health and wellbeing and prolong his life. One of the activities he earmarked to help him do this was to train for a marathon to help him shed the pounds. He may even have tried to encourage himself further by signing up to support his favourite charity through sponsorship on the run.

If he neglected to mention any of this to his family, how would they take his endeavours? All his spouse and children would see is a family member who is around even less because he is 'indulging' in his new obsession of running every day. They may even actively try to stop him, thinking that he may injure himself or cause serious health problems. Yet, different would their reactions be if Joe explained that he was running to get fit, lose weight and support a charity that was tugging at his heart strings? They'd do everything they could to smooth the way. Even if they didn't fully support him, they would be more understanding and not get in the way.

The same goes for a corporate situation, if not more so. Returning to our fictitious Acme Web Corp (AWC), as we have already seen, the company owner has set out to more than double turnover, from £6 million now to £15 million in three years. This target, which is onerous by anyone's standards, involves a complete change in the way the company operates.

Companies that set ambitious growth targets like this are sometimes reticent about telling their team about them. They believe that, if they make an announcement like 'We are going to double turnover in three years', the natural reaction on the shop floor will be disbelief and resentment. In the mind's eye of the AWC directors, the staff members are already muttering: 'We're turning over £6 million already, isn't that enough? How much do they need? Surely they are just being greedy.'

Yet, what the company bosses are relying upon to make this judgement is a perception, not the reality. Just because a company is growing and making more money doesn't automatically mean that the workers will want a large cut of the excess and will become a disruptive force if they don't receive it. When a large PLC announces billions in profits and a £2 million bonus for its chief executive, it is rare to hear employees say they are not going to do any more work from now on because they are only being paid £30,000. If employees really did have that attitude, a company wouldn't want them working for it because they would not be supporters of the business.

Conversely, if the team is kept in the dark, they may not know that AWC has debts of more than £1 million and is barely making any profit out of its £6 million sales. In the absence of any other information, all they'll be able to hang on to is the £6 million figure, which will give them a totally false impression of the company's true status.

In the worst-case scenario, those who don't understand what you are trying to do may even become terrorists against your cause and try to throw the business off kilter, or stop the growth plan completely before it has a chance to get off the ground.

If you are running a company and want to increase turnover substantially, or move the business to the next stage in any other way, you have to get the team on board. You cannot let fear of failure or of lack of support from the team stop you from telling them. Remember, deciding *not* to do something is as much a decision as deciding to do it. Make sure you make the right decision, and the right decision every time is to try to take everyone with you.

People want to be part of a winning team. It's great to be part of something exciting and dynamic. If you'd like to – not because you feel you have to – you could add in the carrot of a reward of a company trip abroad, or a bonus, if the target is met.

Just telling people what you are trying to achieve will help you take a huge step forward. Once you have explained clearly to people what their roles will be in this three-year plan and what will be expected of them at each step along the way, you'll be motoring along together.

Be precise in your instructions, but also allow a certain amount of leeway. I've always rather liked the Disney model, in which each member of the team is charged with 'creating a magic moment' every single day. New recruits may think something like, 'How is that possible? I'm just a hotel room cleaner – I never even see a customer.' But they, like everyone, are shown a way through the example of others in the team who have been inspired to come up with innovative ways to create magic moments. Thus, if you stay in a Disney resort hotel, you may well come back to your room to find your kids' cuddly toys lined up in front of the TV watching the Disney channel. A magic moment indeed.

Tell your team about your plan and what needs to be done, but give them enough room and encouragement to contribute their own ideas on how to get there. They will probably surprise you.

You must also accept that, even if you fully include those around you in your ambitious three-year plan, there is a chance that not everyone will buy into it. Indeed, if your plan is as ambitious as it should be, there is a good chance that most people will have slight reservations about whether it can be done. They may even think you are off your rocker to even imagine something so huge. You have to be prepared for this sort of reaction because the type of growth we are talking about here is abnormal and way beyond what most people can imagine for themselves. People may find it hard to relate to you at all. That is fine and even understandable. It is up to you to convince them that you can and will make it happen and if possible get them on board.

Not everyone will automatically support you, even after this. Some people will never be able to see beyond the thought that you are crazy to even consider doing what you are doing. Your chances of getting there are zero, they will laugh, shaking their heads.

Do you know what? I am delighted when that happens! Someone telling me that I can't do something gives me a power and energy like no other. It makes me more determined than ever to reach my goal – in double-quick time if possible – just to prove them wrong. At the same time, though, this person will have instantly proved that they are not the right person to come along on my fantastic journey. It may be time for a fair and honest parting of the ways.

### Who is on the bus?

Legendary General Electric CEO Jack Welch lived by his philosophy that 10 per cent of a company's worst performers should be culled every year while the top 20 per cent should be made to feel as loved as a close member of the family. The thinking behind his theory is that the top 20 per cent of people are the most productive, the middle 70 per cent work OK and the bottom 10 per cent are essentially non-performers.

Welch's theory is not without its critics, who claim the rule is too arbitrary and introduces a destructive level of uncertainty that sours everyone's performance, from the top to the bottom. However, the bare fact is that this so-called rank-and-yank system coincided with a 28-fold increase in earnings over the time Welch was at General Electric's helm (between 1981 and 2001).

I am fully in favour of Welch's theory. Indeed, I would strongly advise you to look closely at your team right now to see who is aboard for the exciting ride towards your three-year goal. We all have people around us who are energy sappers or non-performers and now is the perfect time to review their position.

The bottom 10 per cent of any team is easy to spot. If I told you to list the worst-performing 10 per cent of those around you, your mind would go straight to the people in question, before I'd even got the sentence out. You'd immediately know it is Fred, Jamal and Liz.

The harsh truth is that these people should not be aboard your bus for the journey towards your future state – indeed, arguably they never have been. If you want to keep moving towards your ideal future, you must now consider carefully whether these people are capable of helping you get there in the time you have set out. If they are not, you know what you must do.

It is a tough choice, but you may even be doing the 10 per cent group a favour. If you think of them as being in that group, you will never truly trust and respect them and will not exploit their full potential. If you let them go, they will almost certainly thrive in a company elsewhere, because everyone can be amazing at something – they just need to find the right niche.

If you do find yourself parting company with the bottom echelons of your team, do it well. My philosophy has always been that, if it doesn't work out with a member of my team, it is down to me and my company because we recruited them. I've always paid double the going rate of redundancy and given people all the encouragement I could to go on and be amazing elsewhere.

Stay focused and concentrate on your goals. Surround yourself with people who will help and encourage you to reach these goals. Make every activity count and you will accomplish everything you seek.

## Summary
- Do not confuse activity with accomplishment.
- Decide which activities contribute to your plan and focus on them.
- Enrol other people to help when you can't do it all yourself.
- Part company with, or limit your exposure to, people who are unwilling or unable to support you.

### ADDITIONAL PPA EXERCISE

Your reaction to the stress of the work and hours involved in meeting your goals will vary considerably according to your personality type. Some people thrive on pressure, whether they are aware of it or not, and will often deliberately let projects build up to a stage where they can swerve in at the last moment and solve the problem. Others have to tackle things for a set time each day in order to be sure in their own minds that they can get through the activities marked on their transition.

This section will give you some clues to understand how you are reacting to what you have read so far, in accordance with your personality type. It also gives some ideas on how you may best use this chapter for your own style of thinking and learning.

#### Dominance messages
- Busyness does not equal effectiveness.

- Focus all your energies on those activities that contribute to your future plan.
- You may not be able to do everything yourself, so be prepared to delegate.
- Don't be held back by people who are unwilling or unable to support you.

## Influence messages

- Filling your diary does not automatically deliver outcomes.
- Eliminate meetings and activities that do not contribute to your future plan.
- Choose others, based on their relevant competences, to do what you cannot do.
- Part company with non-contributors so that they can go and be amazing elsewhere.

## Steadiness messages

- Review your established work processes to remove unnecessary tasks.
- Eliminate peripheral activities and focus on those that contribute to your future plan.
- Delegate to people you can trust.
- Don't let misplaced loyalty get in the way of removing non-contributors.

## Compliance messages

- Work smarter, not harder, and recognise when perfection may be surplus to requirements.
- Identify your key activities and focus on them.
- When you can't do everything yourself, choose people with appropriate competences.
- Set clear expectations and remove people who fail to meet them.

fbs@mikegreene.co.uk

## CHAPTER SEVEN

# PRESS THE PAUSE BUTTON

*Frustration is beautiful if you use it*

British wartime prime minister Winston Churchill is reported to have once told a journalist that one of the secrets to his success was that he took time out every day to think.

'But we all think about things every day,' the perplexed journalist stammered in reply.

'That's just it though, my dear, we don't,' countered the statesman with characteristic self-assurance.

Even when World War Two was at its peak and the demands on Churchill's time were endless, he insisted on a quiet hour each day in which to think and reflect. He had the typewriters in the Cabinet War Rooms specially modified to deaden the noise of the keys as the secretaries worked away, so nothing would distract him from his meditations. He demanded total silence while he considered the complex events of the day.

If you think about it (and please excuse the pun), we don't often really think about things very much. It is all too easy to get swept up in day-to-day events and not pause for a second to consider how things are going. This is doubly so in the case of a rapid transformation like the one we are discussing in this book. When you are completely focused on a goal, it is hard to look up and see what else is going on around you.

Yet, without pausing regularly to examine yourself and the wider circumstances around your single-minded pursuit of your goals, your entire venture can and will hold some real dangers. As I detailed in chapter four, if you are so focused on your goal that you don't look up regularly to check you are still on track towards your destination, it's easy to veer off track.

If you don't think deeply enough about what is going on around you, you may create your own reality in which you find excuses for things that don't quite add up and stick with them without analysing them. I saw a perfect example of this at a conference I attended not long ago. The event was for people in the newspaper and magazine business and you didn't need to be in the room long to realise the prognosis didn't seem good. Speaker after speaker got to his or her feet to bemoan the state of the industry.

'Consumers just don't read magazines any more,' they cried. 'It is all about electronic media and half the content is free.'

'We can't compete any more,' said another.

'What is the point, when profit margins are so thin?' added another angst-fuelled speaker.

To my joy, in the afternoon, one of my former colleagues finally took the stand and delivered a hard-hitting speech that to me immediately got right to the heart of the matter.

'Love me or hate me, but I am going to tell you the truth,' he boomed. 'I've heard what you've been saying and it is absolute codswallop.'

The audience looked stunned, but that didn't stop my colleague explaining exactly what he meant.

'In reality, yes we are in recession and the market is changing,' he went on. 'But so is every other market and yet some sectors are up 18 per cent year on year. They could just as easily bemoan the internet and the economy, but they don't. They've sat down, thought it through and worked out a way to do well.

'All you are doing with all this moaning is creating your own reality and justifying to yourself a failure you are in the process of creating. You need to sit up and look around you and give some thought as to your place in it all.'

He was absolutely right. The great and the good of this industry were so focused on the goal of growing sales and market share that they didn't pause to look at the wider picture. They knew there were threats, such as a boom in free online content as well as a general economic slowdown, but they weren't drilling down into the issues to see whether they could be made to work to their advantage.

It's not just deep concentration on our goals that stops us from pausing every now and again, either. There is another, more troubling, possibility as to why we often fail to think too deeply about what we are doing. Keeping your head down gives you the perfect 'excuse' to somehow ignore failures and slip-ups along the way. It is almost as if your subconscious is telling you that, if you don't think about it properly, it can't really be happening, so press on regardless because things will sort themselves out.

It's human nature. Not thinking about things, or not admitting they are happening, is a fall-back position for when you don't really want to face up to the fact you've got something wrong. Or to the fact that you are no closer to realising what you've set out to do. Or to the fact that you are not quite as good as you thought you were at something.

I saw this tendency at its most extreme a few years back, when I watched a TV documentary that interviewed death-row inmates in American jails. Without exception, the prisoners refused to accept responsibility for what they had done. They didn't want to think about their appalling crimes too deeply, so they said things like 'It wasn't my fault, I heard voices in my head' or 'My girlfriend made me do it' or 'With my background it is no surprise that I ended up killing someone.'

No one was prepared to face up to what they had done, or the consequences thereof.

It's hard to face up to your actions, particularly when they are as terrible and life-changing as committing a capital crime, but clearly the people on this show were not even prepared to *begin* looking at their lives in this way.

Thankfully, it is unlikely that anyone reading this book will have to face up to anything even approaching such major events; nevertheless, reflecting on what we have done, where we have been and where we are going is something we must all do on a regular basis.

It doesn't do anyone any good to just ignore the bad stuff and brush it under the carpet. All this means is that things don't get done.

### Introduce daily checks

Like that great leader Churchill, we all need to press the pause button *at least* once a day to give our journey, its goals and any obstacles on the way some informed reflection.

It is amazing how much clarity and focus you can get out of thinking. Even if you press the pause button for just 20 minutes a day, it will give you time to concentrate on specific issues and listen to what your instinct is telling you, rather than crashing on regardless.

## QUICK EXERCISE

### The hockey stick of success

When the going gets tough, as it will, you need to find a way of constantly reminding yourself why you are going through all this pain and discomfort. You must keep thinking about your very specific transition goals because, if you don't, you won't have the drive and resilience to get through the tough times.

It might help to look at Figure 15, which I call the hockey stick of success. Imagine, for the sake of argument, that one of your transition goals is to dramatically increase your handicap at golf. For example, you may have a handicap of six or seven and be aiming for a one.

One day, you are playing a round and the ultimate mentor comes along: Tiger Woods!

'I've been watching you play and you've got potential,' says Tiger, walking up with a friendly smile and an outstretched hand. 'I've got a spare hour – would you like some tips?'

Of course, no one in their right mind would turn down such an incredible offer. You willingly follow him to the first tee. In the next hour he shows you new ways to stand, grip your clubs and watch the ball. Everything. It is, without a doubt, one of the most exciting and informative hours of your life.

In the following days and weeks, you try to replicate everything you saw and heard that day. Unfortunately, as is invariably the case when you want to make such huge leaps in performance, you will actually get worse, at least in the short term, while you struggle to perfect what you've learned. You will find it hard to replicate all the new moves, and for a while it won't feel at all natural. Your previous handicap of six or seven may even rise to ten.

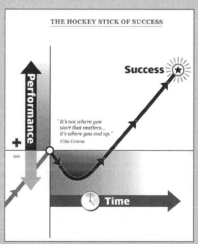

Figure 15

The real danger is that, if you don't properly think about what has been happening, you'll eventually snap and revert to your old way of playing. If you think about this back-track at all, there will probably be some self-justification – you might tell yourself that Tiger Woods didn't really understand your game after all.

If you had just paused to think more deeply, though, you would have realised that you were on the verge of a breakthrough. Most of the time you will have no idea when that breakthrough will come, but it will. It is no good being given an amazing opportunity if you squander it by hiding behind your failure and ignoring what is really happening.

Taking time to meditate and reflect is the key to identifying when there is an upside when all around you seems bleak.

While you should make it a habit to pause and mentally check your plan at least once a day, you would also be advised to physically go over it in detail at least once a month and preferably once a week. A great technique for doing this and to help you drill down into how you are doing is to 'traffic-light' each task. Taking each element one at a time, rate it in either green, amber or red, according to how far you have got in achieving it. Green means that the task has been achieved, amber means that you are on the way and/or on track but still have some way to go, and red means that you have barely started, or failed to achieve that particular goal on your first attempt. To concentrate the mind, you could use stickers or highlighters to actually mark your map.

Traffic-lighting your transition map is a great visual reminder of what needs to be done and, believe me, there is no more satisfying feeling than turning one of the elements from red to green. If people are working on the transition alongside you, it is also a useful way to concentrate their thoughts and keep them on task. No one wants to be responsible for a never-changing sea of red lights! Of course, if you are faced with a flood of green lights, it is a clear signal that you need to up the ante further and put in some more challenging tasks. You would certainly need to re-examine your future-state goals in this instance.

I have included AWC's chart with traffic-light colours marked on it in Figure 16 as an example, but this technique will work equally well for Joe's map and for your own personal transition.

We are now over half way through this book. It has introduced you to a process that will guide you towards your final desired destination. To date you have:

- defined what success means to you in real, detailed terms
- looked at and shed the labels that you have been given erroneously during your life
- worked to get yourself a mentor to help you through this process
- devised strategies to keep you focused on the right direction
- perfected tactics to stop yourself becoming discouraged when things don't seem to be going to plan
- learned to recognise and appreciate the little things that are driving you towards your goal.

Now is the time to press pause and reflect on what you have done so far. To do this, you need to learn a new technique, which will serve to keep you on track every single day.

To draw an analogy, this part of the process is like the daily checks you would make on a high-performance car. The manufacturers of such vehicles advise that you look your vehicle over every day to make sure the oil, water and tyre pressures are at their best. This is the way to ensure optimum performance and trouble-free motoring. In chapter nine, we will look at the equivalent of the annual service, which will draw all these things together and move you on to the next level, but for now let's just take one thing at a time.

If you were to miss one of your daily checks on a high-performance car, it would almost definitely keep running. Even if you missed two or three inspections, it would probably run no differently for a while. Over time, though, this neglect would have an effect. You might not notice any difference if the oil levels were a bit low or the tyres a little deflated, but bit by bit things would be going awry. Eventually, if you continued in this way, your car would need some serious attention and the engine might even need a complete rebuild, which would mean starting again from scratch.

The point of this analogy is as follows: it only takes a few minutes a day to mentally check things over in your life plan, but this is, without a shadow of a doubt, always time well spent towards reaching your long-term goal. Spending time reflecting on what is happening in your strategy, including what might be going wrong, is the key to reaching your goal in the timescale you've set out.

### Meditation – or, thinking about stuff

My guess is that, if I introduce the word 'meditation' here, a good number

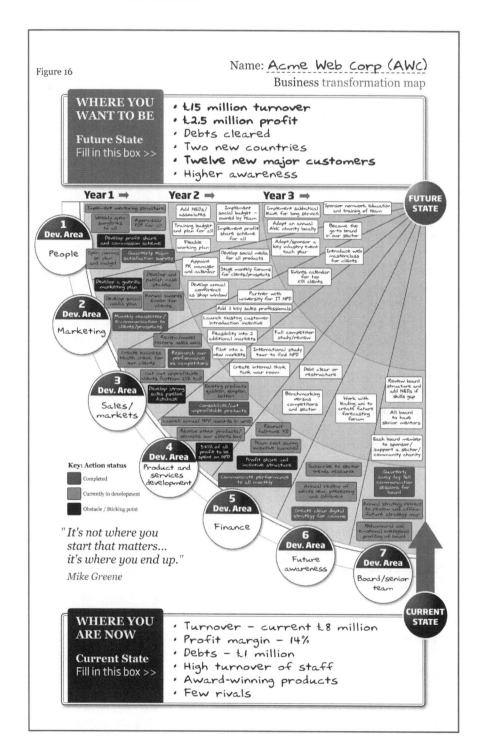

Figure 16

Name: **Acme Web Corp (AWC)**
Business transformation map

**WHERE YOU WANT TO BE**

**Future State**
Fill in this box >>

- £15 million turnover
- £2.5 million profit
- Debts cleared
- Two new countries
- **Twelve new major customers**
- Higher awareness

*"It's not where you start that matters... it's where you end up."*
Mike Greene

**WHERE YOU ARE NOW**

**Current State**
Fill in this box >>

- Turnover – current £8 million
- Profit margin – 14%
- Debts – £1 million
- High turnover of staff
- Award-winning products
- Few rivals

of readers are going to slam the book shut and say they've had enough of this New Age twaddle – it's not for them. So, for the sake of linguistics and if it helps, you can call the reflections we are about to do 'thinking about stuff'.

If you train your mind to think about stuff, it will show you the hurdles that are blocking your way to becoming the successful you. You will be able to light up a clear path to resolving these issues because your mind will be relaxed and focused. Knowing how to approach things in this way means you will be able to devote your complete attention to the matter in hand and ultimately be more creative in the solution.

Once you have learned techniques that will enable you to clear your mind of everyday thoughts and stresses and become more focused, you will be amazed at how clearly you will see what lies ahead and what, if any, adjustments need to be made.

How do we do this? Well, one day at a time. Literally. We need to get into the habit of pinpointing one area of our plan *each day* that needs more reflection. Thinking deeply about a specific problem on a day-by-day basis will help you to understand it better, deal with your thoughts and emotions around it and lead you to a calm, rational response.

There are many ways to press the pause button and think about stuff, but the two we will discuss here are 'guided meditation' and 'spot meditation'. Generally, it takes a little longer to master and practice guided meditation, so I'll tackle that first. Spot meditation is a technique you will be able to learn once you've become more experienced at guided meditation. It will enable you to put yourself into a meditative state for just a few moments in order to tackle problems as and when they come up. Both methods are very effective and they can, in fact, work in tandem with one another.

**Guided meditation**
Guided meditation is a form of meditation in which you are guided into a beneficial state of consciousness by someone else. That someone else doesn't need to be a real person in the room with you; it could be a voice recording. There are hundreds of free audio-guided meditations online, as well as easy-to-follow examples on video-sharing websites such as YouTube. Many are specific meditations towards targets such as boosting your self-esteem, reducing anxiety about specific issues, dealing with anger, overcoming procrastination, or even learning new skills. Experiment with a few that are specific to your own aims to find one you are comfortable with, or ring the changes by trying out different ones each time.

In guided meditation, you follow verbal cues to help you relax your entire body, clear your mind, concentrate on breathing and focus your awareness and attention. To do a proper guided meditation, you will need to sit somewhere quietly for between five and twenty minutes a day – although, if you do have more time, it is well worth devoting it to exploring the possibilities of thought more deeply.

The secret to meditation lies in developing, focusing and directing your own awareness. Bear in mind that there is no 'right' or 'wrong' way to meditate. Whatever you experience should be right for you. Don't try to force anything to happen. The following simple breathing exercise is a great starting point.

- Find a quiet place in which to comfortably sit or lie down. Try to find a position in which you won't drop off to sleep too easily.
- Close your eyes and roll your shoulders slowly forward and then slowly back.
- Lean your head from side to side, lowering your right ear towards your right shoulder and then your left ear towards your left shoulder.
- Relax and begin to observe your breathing. Don't try to change it – just notice as your breath flows in and out.
- When your attention begins to wander – as it will – gently focus it back on your breath flowing in and out of your body. Notice your stray thoughts, but don't dwell on them.
- Focus on the stages of a complete breath. There is the in breath, a slight pause, an exhalation and then another pause before a further in breath.
- Think about your breathing more deeply. Feel the air enter through your nose, and picture it flowing through the cavities in your sinuses and deep down into your lungs.
- See, in your mind's eye, the air inside your body, filling it gently.
- Notice how your lungs seem to become smaller after you breathe out.
- Become aware of your chest and stomach rising and falling on each breath.
- Now begin to count silently between each inhalation and exhalation.
- Inhale, count one.
- Exhale, count one.
- Inhale, one.
- Exhale, one.
- Continue doing this, counting each action as one.
- Pause.
- How do you feel? Your breathing should be calm and gentle and your body should feel relaxed.
- To come out of the meditation, you must gently reawaken your body

and mind. Begin by noticing the sounds around you and feeling the ground beneath your body.

- Wiggle your fingers and toes.
- Then, shrug your shoulders and stretch out your arms and legs.
- When you feel ready, open your eyes, but stay sitting for a few moments more.
- Stretch your legs and arms again and pause to enjoy how relaxed you feel as your body reawakens and returns to its usual state of alertness.
- Slowly stand up and silently celebrate your new feeling of energy and alertness.

As you become more adept at guided meditation, you will be able to follow specific guided meditations to help with just about any situation. Just search online as and when you identify an area of your life that needs some attention.

Once you have given yourself the space and time, you will find that a few moments of carefully guided thought will be able to solve just about any problem and get you back on the right track. As I have said many times already, the brain has an infinite ability to give you all the responses and guidance you need. You just need to know how to ask the right questions of it. To go back to the taxi-driver analogy, it is like asking your driver to pull over into a lay-by for a moment to check whether there is a better route to your destination. The chances are that there will be.

### Spot meditation

It is not always essential to spend 20 minutes sitting with your eyes closed in order to meditate effectively. Although I would certainly recommend getting into the habit of regularly putting your consciousness into a deep state in order to really get to the core of what is going on, it is equally important to be able to turn to these skills as and when you need them throughout the day. Besides which, however hard you try (and you should try very hard indeed), you won't always have the luxury of 20 or so uninterrupted minutes every day.

There is a shorter meditative technique called 'spot meditation'. Spot meditation can take up as little as a few seconds of your time, certainly no more than a minute or so. Once you get good at it, you'll soon find that with a few well-placed spot meditations you're racking up 20 minutes of good thinking time a day and you will have barely interrupted your schedule. (The great thing about perfecting this technique is that it takes away the excuse that you simply don't have time to think – you can zoom in and do a spot meditation in a matter of seconds.)

Even if you are in the midst of a stressful day, or perhaps especially because you are in the midst of a stressful day, there are always punctuation points you can use more effectively. These moments could be:

- travelling to and from work
- while you are waiting in a queue in the shop, or at a café counter
- in the shower or toilet
- when you are walking somewhere
- when you are put on hold during a phone call
- while waiting for internet pages to load.

In all these seemingly mundane and occasionally frustrating activities, there are opportunities to take your mind to another place by concentrating on sensory things. You could switch your attention to the air you are breathing, the song being played while you're on hold or an emotion you are feeling. By doing this, you will be taking your mind away from the things that stir you up about what may or may not happen in the future, or your anger over what has gone by. It will strip away the tension and clear your thoughts. This is all you need to do to get into a meditative state.

There are many examples of techniques for spot meditation and, again, the internet is a good resource to turn to in order to find examples. The best way to perfect spot meditation is to choose one method that works for you and stick to it for a while until it becomes second nature.

One of my favourite spot meditations is called 'red light' and, as the name suggests, it is to do with the time you spend in your car sitting at a traffic light as you wait for the green signal. This may seem like a frustrating waste of time, but it is as good a time as any to get your mind into a better place, because there is not a lot else you can do for those few seconds.

A red-light spot meditation goes something like this:

- Relax. Shrug your shoulders and shake your arms loose.
- Settle back in the seat and take three or four deep breaths.
- Mentally scan your body for signs of tension. How, for example, are you holding the steering wheel? Are your knuckles white with tension?
- Are your face and neck muscles relaxed? Soften them.
- What about your stomach?
- Keep breathing. Think about the present. Look around you slowly. See the scenery around you, the traffic and the flora and fauna at the edge of the road.
- When the lights turn green, the exercise is over and it is time to devote your attention to the task in hand, which is driving safely.

Now that I've become proficient at my red-light spot meditation, I sometimes up the ante and, after getting into a meditative state, give my subconscious the next 30 seconds to give me an answer to a question that is troubling me. It's amazing how well this works.

Hopefully, having got this far in the book, you will at least consider trying some form of meditation in order to raise your consciousness concerning what is going on both within you and on the outside.

Call it what you like – whether pressing the pause button, thinking about stuff or meditating – this is a great way to tackle problems and things that trouble you. Even tasks that seem insurmountable at first sight will seem more manageable once you have given them some thinking time. I always liken the aftereffects of my own thinking time to that photography trick whereby, using perspective, you can make the subject appear to be holding up a well-known landmark such as the Eiffel Tower or the Houses of Parliament in the palm of their hand. If you step away from anything and look at it in a different way, suddenly it will seem much smaller and easier to manage. Meditating on an issue will make you think differently about it. You will feel bigger and more in control.

## QUICK EXERCISE

### Stretch yourself

I'd like you to do something for me. Wherever you are sitting now, place both hands in the air. Now, I'd like you to reach up as far as you can go. Really stretch yourself. Good. I guess you think that is as far as you can reach?

Now, I'd like you to see if you can reach a further two inches into the air. Go on, try it.

There. I bet you've managed it.

What you have just proved is that we all have the capacity to reach a few inches higher, if we really need to. We just need to give it a bit more effort.

Pressing the pause button is a great moment to test our subconscious to see if we are giving our all in pursuit of our goals. As part of your meditations, look at your transition plan as it is now and ask yourself: are you really giving it your all and doing everything you can to reach your desired future state? What could you be doing better?

### Selfish me

You may be concerned that your lifestyle does not really lend itself to a quiet time for reflection each day. It probably seems like there is noise, hustle and bustle going on around you the whole time. The short answer to this is: use these distractions. You are not going to get rid of that noise, so you may as well accept it and, better still, build it in as part of your meditative routine. If you live or work in a built-up area, for example, tell your brain that every car that passes will drive you more deeply into your meditation. And it will. As I have said repeatedly, the brain is programmed to take you anywhere you need to go. This is the time to help it along by giving yourself time to think.

Another of the most common arguments a lot of people will put forward about not being able to stop and think is that they simply don't have the time. It sounds like a great idea but, hey, work, family and this, that and the other have to be taken care of, and snatching a few moments for yourself is a distant dream.

If this sounds like you, you really do need to press the pause button hard and reprioritise. You don't just need daily meditation; you need to make a regular spot in your life for some 'you time' too.

Although I live (and have always lived) a pretty hectic life, I am always sure to make time for myself, to do the things that I want and that interest me. I call it my 'selfish me' time. Whether it is taking some exercise, having a weekend away with the lads or just settling down to read a book, it is part of what makes me me.

Why do I do this? Well, the more you give up in life to meet your responsibilities, the more you give up of yourself. It chips away at you. Then, one day you will wake up and realise you are not enjoying life much at all.

It always drives me crazy when people ask me what is more important to me: work or family. Of course, the answer is family, but to me it is like asking which arm I would like to have cut off. Why should I choose? Both things are part of who I am, just like the things that I do outside the spheres of work and family.

Not taking time for yourself is like trying to make an amazing beef bourguignon and forgetting one of the key ingredients, such as mushrooms. The resulting dish will nourish and sustain you, but it won't be a deeply satisfying meal and just won't seem quite right. It's just the same with a person. If you deplete or weaken the elements that make up the whole self, the person will be harmed in the long term and prevented from achieving his or her goals.

The idea behind 'selfish me' is all about getting balance in your life. It ignores for a moment the fact that you have a partner, kids or a demanding job, or all of the above. It says that, at least once a week, you will do something that is purely for you. Whether it is rambling, playing a team sport or simply going out with friends, it will be something you have chosen for you.

This will help to make up the whole you and will keep your soul nourished and prepared to go on to bigger, more challenging things. Taking time for yourself and time to think is not a luxury, to be left until that mythical moment when you finally 'have time'. It is an essential part of the transformation process. Without it, you cannot hope to reach, or even exceed, your tough goals.

Now, that's worth a few moments' thought, don't you think?

**Summary**
- Build time for thinking, focus and reflection into each day.
- Train your mind (access more of the latent ability of your brain).
- Growth often starts with a step back. Stretch, because you can achieve more.
- Carve out some 'selfish me' time – it's crucial.

## ADDITIONAL PPA EXERCISE

Your reaction to the idea, or even value, of meditation will vary considerably according to your personality type. Some people are very receptive to the idea of a moment or two of reflection to solve a problem, while others prefer to battle on in the belief they can get through it.

This section will give you some clues to understand how you are reacting to what you have read so far, in accordance with your personality type. It also gives some ideas on how you may best use this chapter for your own style of thinking and learning.

### Dominance messages
- Time spent thinking is a necessary investment, not a waste.
- Your brain is an asset to be exploited to its maximum capacity.
- Sometimes a step back can provide the impetus to move forwards more quickly.
- Protect 'selfish me' time to recharge your batteries.

**Influence messages**
- You need time for private reflection without input from others.
- Your brain has huge untapped potential.
- You might need a step back to focus more clearly on where to push yourself.
- Protect 'selfish me' time to keep your spirits up.

**Steadiness messages**
- Never apologise for taking regular time out for reflection.
- Your brain is a resource like any other, and needs to be developed.
- Pressing the pause button allows you to focus on what you could do better.
- Protect 'selfish me' time to keep things in proportion.

**Compliance messages**
- You know how vital it is to allocate time for thoughtful reflection, so schedule it in.
- You need to access the full latent ability of your brain.
- There is always room for improvement and you must stretch yourself to achieve it.
- Protect 'selfish me' time to prevent burnout.

**CHAPTER EIGHT**

## CHANGE YOUR PACK

You are the average of the five people you spend the most time with

– Jim Rohn

In my early teens I was a punk, in every sense of the word. I sported spiky hair, ripped jeans, t-shirts held together with so many safety pins that so you could barely read the loud slogans emblazoned across them and, of course, a trade-mark angry snarl on my face. Me and my mate Stuart, who was the only other punk I knew, used to hang out together all the time. We'd lean casually on various walls around our hometown while we perfected our punk 'attitude', which was an ingenious combination of a menacing, unapproachable air, complete derision concerning anyone who wasn't like us, and total boredom at the mundane existence we all led. Stuart and I prided ourselves on refusing to conform to anything, and that included a refusal to knuckle down to our schoolwork. We were, I am ashamed to say, pretty rude to the teachers who tried to encourage us to study.

Looking back now, I can't believe what an idiot I was. Who was I kidding? As teenage phases go, this was not one to be proud of. In a way, though, I was lucky. This period and what went after it taught me an incredibly valuable lesson. It is a lesson that has stood me in good stead all my adult life.

When I was 15 years old, Stuart and I had a tremendous falling out just before school broke up for the summer holidays. Although the passage of time has ensured that I can no longer remember the reason for this bust-up, I can remember even now that it was the most almighty row and that blows were exchanged. It was one of those quarrels from which there is no turning back and, indeed, we never really spoke to one another again.

So there I was, at the start of the summer break, no longer on speaking terms with my one and only buddy. In my mind's eye, the six-week break seemed to stretch away, far into the distance, because – as you will no doubt recall – when you are young the school summer holidays seem to last forever. What was I going to do with myself?

After a couple of days of kicking my heels, I thought I was going to go mad with boredom. Remember, this was the early eighties, in the days before games consoles and decent daytime telly. There weren't mobile phones either, not that I had anyone to call and invite round. Plus, I wasn't much into books. There just didn't seem anything to do.

'What am I going to do?' I thought to myself. 'I am going out of my mind and I still have six weeks to go.'

Then, my eyes fell upon the mound of holiday work the school had given us to prepare for our O levels in the coming academic year. At the time, when they had handed it over, I had fully intended to leave it in my school bag throughout July and August. Maybe, though – just maybe – it was worth giving it a go.

So, I picked up the schoolbooks and for the first time in years began to really study. I won't say it was the most exciting summer of my life, and a lot of the time I felt really sad and lonely, but at least the time passed pretty rapidly as I revised hard. Many of the things that had not made sense at all in the previous year, when I had not been concentrating, now seemed straight forward. Amazingly, I found within me a hunger for knowledge that I'd never realised I had.

When I got back to school for the autumn term, everyone immediately noticed the change in me. The teachers seemed genuinely pleased that I was finally taking an interest and did all they could to encourage my studies. Plus, as an added bonus for my 15-year-old self, several girls who had previously steered very clear from me approached me to say admiringly how much I had changed for the better. That recognition gave me all the motivation I needed to go on to bigger and better things.

At the end of the year, I notched up eight O levels, with good A- and B-grade passes. I'd never have achieved that, or gone on to further education, if I had remained in my friendship with Stuart. By changing the people I surrounded myself with, or my 'pack', I freed myself from my negative influences and started on a path to transform my future.

We are all part of packs because, like it or not, behaviourally, we human beings have not moved that far away from our ancient ancestors. We were pack animals then and still are. Being accepted as one of the crowd is one of our biggest motivators in life and you can't usually be part of a pack without becoming like the rest of those in the pack. It is a rare human being indeed who is totally self-sufficient and able to live on his or her own. Indeed, most of us are part of several packs, be it family, friends or work colleagues.

Yet, as my story here shows, there are times when it is prudent to change your pack. If you want to change yourself and fulfil your ambitious goals, you must look carefully at the people you surround yourself with. If they do not support you, or even have the capacity to do so, or worse still constantly bring you down to their level, something has to give. If you don't move on, you will not be in control of your destiny.

At its most extreme, this means that, if you hang around with a bunch of drug addicts, the chances are you will eventually go down this path. But, to take a more general example, imagine you hang out with a group of negative people. These may be people who have not learned how to deal with failure, or even considered that they could do something with their lives. Their negative thoughts and beliefs will drag you down. They'll encourage you to believe that nothing is possible and, if you hang around with them long enough, they'll probably be right.

If this sounds like the situation you are in, maybe it is time to change your pack.

To achieve your goals and turn negative energy into positive energy, you have to get away from the naysayers – the people who will encourage you to do anything but fulfil your dreams. People like this will only bring you down, and once you reach a certain depth it can be very hard to bring yourself back up.

The alternative is to seek out a new pack and to surround yourself with positive people, perhaps those who also have the skills and/or experience you need to reach your goals. Such people will improve your life, energise you and make your goals seem attainable. In the course of developing friendships and relationships with people that inspire you, part of their magic will rub off onto you.

Being part of a great pack is a powerful thing.

## Identifying your packs
The quote at the beginning of the chapter is from the American motivational speaker Jim Rohn.[8] He worked out, quite rightly, that the circle of people you spend the most time with have a profound impact on your life. Your pack will determine how you think, the decisions you make and how you act. Ultimately, it would not be an exaggeration to say that it is quite possible that this small group will dictate how successful you will be.

It doesn't matter how clever you are, or how determined, or how talented in a particular field; what will really count in your path to success is the people you are closest to. They will have more of an impact on your fortunes than months of hard work late into the night, or even the combined total of all the motivational ideas you've written on your transition map. If you ignore this stage of the process, you may well grind to a halt at a point that is far short of your goals.

Who knows why we hook up with packs that are not really doing us any good. It doesn't help that the worst packs are the easiest to get into. After all, if, say, you wanted to join the first team for athletics, it would entail hard work to achieve that and then sustain your position. However, if you wanted to get into the B team, C team or even D team, the entry requirements probably wouldn't be that onerous.

If you want to move on, though, you need to identify your pack and work out whether it is the right one for you. You may, as detailed in the previous section, be connected to several packs. What we need to do here is determine which have the most influence over you, whether negative or positive.

## Changing your pack
Although the prospect seems daunting, sometimes changing your pack is actually pretty straight forward. Having scored people around you on a scale, it is easy to see who is dragging you down and you can simply lessen the time you spend with those people. If they are friends, for example, you can just stop calling or not be as available when everyone is arranging a night out. Initially it may seem painful, even rude, but sooner or later you will all move on and get on with your lives. Most of the time that friend will not even realise they've been eased out of the pack. They may just assume it is part of the natural cycle of friendship, in which close acquaintances peak and wane over the years as interests and priorities change.

Other times, it is not quite as easy. You may be so intricately connected with a group that it seems almost impossible to break away. I mentioned

8. Jim Rohn, *Seven Strategies for Wealth and Happiness*. Prima Life, 1996.

## QUICK EXERCISE

## Name your packs

Let's stick with Rohn's assumption that it is just five people who have the most impact on your life. First of all, write down who you judge to be the five who are closest to you. Remember, a day has 24 hours, so these people may include your spouse, family members, work colleagues and/or long-term friends. Indeed, your list may include all of these. Don't tie yourself in knots if you come up with four or six – an approximation is fine.

Now, and this is the tough bit, try to think about these people objectively, as though you were not close to them. Think about who they are, what they do with their own lives and whether they are ambitious, successful or creative. Are they happy and optimistic, or is everything just too much of an effort for them?

Now, write down a score of anything between one to ten against each name. Ten out of ten means that this person is fantastically positive and clearly an asset to your life, helping you towards your goals and generally spurring you on in every way. One out of ten denotes that the person is a disruptive force who distracts you from your vision, whether or not they intend to do so.

The rankings on your list will probably not come as much of a surprise. You already know which of those around you push you forward when you need support and which of them leave you feeling tired, irritable and in need of a lie down. However, seeing it in black and white should help you to see that it is time you did something about your pack.

Tough though it may seem, you need to make a decision about who you will keep in your pack and who has to go. If you are brave and determined enough to do this, you may only be left with two, or perhaps even fewer, from your original pack. However, this is what needs to be done if you are determined to meet the challenges you've been setting out for yourself throughout this book. Right now, this may seem too difficult, and we'll come to some suggestions as to how to ease the process in the next section. In the meantime, though, to add some grist to the mill, remember that this is not a journey that you embarked upon lightly. Throughout this book I have urged you to think big and then, even when you have some pretty meaty goals, to challenge yourself to stretch even further. Well, big goals require big determination. No one said it would be easy and now is the time to really test your mettle.

If you find yourself wavering, consider Rohn's argument that 'you earn the average of the salaries of the five people you spend the most time with.'[1]

So, if your ambition is to be a millionaire, live comfortably and retire by the age of 55, how likely is this to happen if you go round with five friends who all earn an average of £30,000? Of course, it would be pushing the realms of plausibility to suggest that in attempting to change your pack you could hook up with people earning £250,000-plus overnight. However, how open will you be to progressing towards this goal if you are constantly surrounded by people who are nowhere close to it?

It is time to be honest with yourself. If you are not willing to examine and potentially change your pack, or to go through the pain of the exercise, how serious are you about your goal? I never said this process would be easy, and it isn't. The question you need to answer is: how much do you want it to happen?

1. As quoted in: Randy Gage, 'Mindset maintenance'. *Prosperity Blog*, undated. www.randygage.com/blog/mindset-maintenance.

my brother Leroy in chapter one and how much I admired his home-grown version of success. What I haven't said was that what first inspired his thirst for adventure was an equally strong desire to get away from the circle of friends who surrounded him in his early twenties. To put it politely, they were a bunch of ne'er-do-wells who could easily have pulled him down into a lifetime of hard drinking, drug-taking and who knows what. Luckily Leroy had the presence of mind to realise this and the inner strength to do something about it. He knew he did not want to embrace the negative labels his friends had so easily adopted, but at the same time he realised the only way to get away from this was to completely move away from the district. So, he left the pack and started travelling. Leroy had to change his geography in order to be free of this pack. He did and it transformed his life, enabling him to fulfil all his goals.

Another less-than-straight-forward scenario is when a member of your pack works for you. If you run your own business, you'll recognise this scenario straight away. There will be one person who is just never happy, however much you do for them. Their relentless sniping may really drag you and other members of the team down.

I had just this problem in my business once. This fellow, let's call him Phil, started off as an excellent worker. Nothing was too much trouble and, if anyone was needed to go the extra mile, Phil was always the first to step forward. He was loyal, too, and had been with the company for 15 years when we first noticed things were going awry.

Slowly but surely, his performance started to wane. He seemed tired, grumpy and distracted. I stepped in quickly to see what the problem was and Phil explained he was feeling a bit bored. He joked that he was having a mid-life crisis and asked whether we would bear with him. I said that we would do more than that and would endeavour to present him with some fresh challenges to boost his interest. Nothing seemed to hit the mark, though, and his period in the doldrums continued. It was obvious Phil was beginning to become a very disruptive influence indeed.

Finally, in desperation, we agreed with Phil's request to move out to Australia to work in our office there. If he had been working with his former fervour and diligence, he would have been an incredible asset in our venture down under. Sadly, though, he was still bored and quickly decided that Australia was not for him after all.

When Phil returned to the UK, I could see I had some real thinking to do. He couldn't settle at anything and was becoming an unintentional saboteur within the company. From being in the top 10 per cent of the employees, he had slipped to the bottom 10 per cent and nothing we did could raise him up again. Phil had to go. He could no longer be part of my work pack.

This may sound harsh, but I would rather move someone on with a handsome payoff than leave him there disrupting the rest of the business. To use a blunt analogy, Phil had become like a cancerous growth, festering within my team. This growth had to be cut out for the long-term health of my company and the wellbeing of the others who relied on it for their livelihoods.

We treated Phil well, giving him a higher-than-average redundancy package and an excellent reference. He was not surprised by the turn of events. He knew things had not been going well. We'd been talking for months about how his work had gone off the boil.

In the end, the situation turned out well for all concerned. After a period of rest, Phil got another job and is now thriving at another company. In fact, he is back to his usual hard-working, dedicated self. He is happier, too, and glad that things turned out as they did. As for my business, we carried on with a new spring in our step because someone who clearly didn't want to be there was no longer dragging us down. Changing the pack was the right thing to do for everyone.

What, though, do you do if the negative pack influence comes from members of your own family? This presents a whole new set of problems because it is virtually impossible to cut ties with your immediate family, no matter how difficult the relationship. Indeed, as I know from a close friend who fosters children, blood is always thicker than water. It doesn't seem to matter how badly some youngsters are physically and mentally abused by their parents, they will always do their utmost to return to the family home. The bond is so strong, it is virtually impossible to break.

If you are in a situation in which you recognise that your family is the pack you most need to change, it is tough one. If you are determined to take this path, and you will have to be, you have little alternative but to try to limit the amount of time you spend with them. Don't try to cut them out of your life completely because you won't succeed. If possible, keep face-to-face time to a minimum, perhaps just special occasions such as Christmas and birthdays. You may be able to save face by moving away physically for a while and 'blaming' geography for your lack of appearance. It is a strategy I adopted at the age of 19, when I started looking carefully at my pack following my experience with Stuart. I knew there were difficulties at home that were holding me back and I deliberately accepted a job as a relief manager travelling all over the country because I knew that it would take me away from home for two or three months. That was the break I needed to get out from under my family's influence; the physical distance gave me the space to think more clearly.

There is a certain amount of protection that comes from the fact that you have recognised the negative influence your family pack has upon you and have made a conscious decision to overcome it. This knowledge will form an imaginary force field around you and will give you strength to bear their negative behaviour.

If you are not able to physically remove yourself, you could break free by using a healthy dose of self-belief. One good method is to stand back and think more objectively about the family member who is affecting you so badly. If, for example, this person is undermining your ability to meet any of your goals, ask yourself whether he or she is qualified to judge, just as you did in chapter two when we considered the negative labels that people erroneously give you. What does your mother know about running a successful company? What does your brother know about being a multi-millionaire? By all means love them for who they are and what they do know, but be

---

### QUICK EXERCISE

## Be positive

You've probably heard the expression 'misery loves company'. Well, positivity does too. This is a useful thing to remember when you are taking big leaps of faith, such as changing your pack. If you remain positive, even when times are tough, people will be drawn to you.

So, next time someone moans to you about the awful weather you've been having, smile breezily and say it's liquid sunshine! If someone bemoans the dreadful economic climate, point out all the companies that you know that are thriving. You will naturally attract other positive people around you (and these are the people you need to surround yourself with) while the negative ones will see that they get no traction from you and will go elsewhere. Job done!

---

confident enough in your plans to recognise that you are the best person to judge things from your own perspective when it comes to your ambitions.

### It will be tough

A complete change of pack is unusual because it is a very painful thing to do. Although I eventually received much praise and recognition for my teenage reinvention after I stopped being a rude punk and knuckled down to studying, it didn't happen overnight. Even today I remember how lonely and wretched I felt over the summer holiday as I toiled over my books. When I was at my lowest point, I'm pretty sure that, if my mate Stuart had come knocking on my door, I'd have gladly gone right back to being that obnoxious, lazy kid. I felt so dreadful that anything would have been better. Plus, right then, I had no way of knowing for sure whether my new attitude would turn out to my advantage with great exam results and the recognition and friendship of my peers.

With the benefit of hindsight, it is clearly one of the best moves I ever made. However, getting over that fear and uncertainty requires a big leap of faith. Remember the hockey stick exercise from the last chapter: there will be a trough before you begin to see the positive effects of change. For a while, all in the garden will definitely not seem rosy.

Accepting that you will be worse off can seem counter-intuitive, particularly if the scale of the task ahead seems so large and daunting that it is virtually impossible. This is where your transition map comes into play. If you are absolutely clear about what you want and where you want to be, you won't let yourself get distracted by your doubts and fears. You already know it is going to be painful, but at the same time can see why you are putting yourself through the mill.

Occasionally, you may need to take a very big leap of faith indeed to change your pack. Let me give you an example. Not long ago, as part of my mentoring activities, I was working with a large manufacturing group. The company had contracts all over the world, but it was haemorrhaging cash and staff turnover was terrible. After the briefest of conversations with the key personnel and a quick scan of the books, it was immediately obvious why. This company was losing money hand over fist with its largest customer.

It had become a victim of that classic business syndrome in which a company will bend over backwards to please one demanding customer, so much so that it turns into a damaging and wealth-destroying relationship. Every business instinct screams against the idea, but, if you are running a company like this, the pack that needs to be got rid of is the customer.

In the case of the company I was mentoring, the manufacturer had pitched for the business five years earlier and had been cock-a-hoop when the customer had said they'd like to work with them. However, there were conditions. The manufacturer had originally quoted, say, £1 million per annum for the job, but the customer said that if they dropped their price by 25 per cent they'd get the contract. The customer had added the sweetener that the manufacturer would be put in pole position for some other work that was going to be out for tender shortly. Imagining that a lucrative relationship was developing, the manufacturer agreed and work began.

Of course, while the manufacturer had agreed to a 25 per cent reduction in the price, there was no way the customer would accept a 25 per cent reduction in the level of servicing of their account, or in the quality of the goods. Indeed, being a large company and acutely aware of their prestige in the industry, they wanted their account to be over-serviced. They demanded that the account directors who looked after the account put at least 25 per cent *more* time and effort into the account than was normal and that the quality of the product should be absolutely first class. The manufacturer was now in a situation in which it was running an account that should have been billing £1.25 million a year but only pulling in £750,000. That is quite a disparity.

To make matters worse, despite negotiating hard for an annual inflation-linked increase, the manufacturer actually became even worse off year by year. After all, a 3 per cent rise in a fee of £750,000 is £22,500, whereas 3 per cent of £1.25 million is £37,500. Adding insult to injury, the promised extra work to alleviate the blow of the initial fee cut never materialised.

Everyone was fed up. The directors of the manufacturer felt helpless because they were losing money. Their staff were unmotivated and depressed because they were working their socks off but not getting anywhere. Even those who were not working on the account felt downhearted about working for a company that was clearly not getting anywhere.

'This is an abusive client,' I told them. 'You've got to get rid of them.'

The directors looked shocked.

'But this is one of the most prestigious companies in the field,' they exclaimed. 'We're lucky to have them on the books. It gives us a lot of prestige.'

I then had to explain to them why this was not the case. Being in this company's pack was rapidly destroying the manufacturer's business. Not only were they losing money every year but they were losing good staff too. Plus, in reality it meant very little to have this great name on the books. Indeed, it actually meant that rival companies would not work with the manufacturer for competitive reasons – and these rival companies would have paid the going rate.

Finally, I told the directors that, if the company got a reputation as one that was prepared to cut its costs in order to keep a client, its position in the industry would become very perilous indeed.

'It will be painful,' I said. 'Turning down that much income will feel like it leaves a giant hole in your finances. No one ever likes to turn business away.' However, I explained that this was a strategy I always ruthlessly pursued in my own businesses. When I did, at least eight times out of ten my customers returned to me after a year or so – and they always agreed to pay the full rate.

'If you are good at what you do, have the courage of your convictions,' I said. 'Politely let the customer go and get on with growing the business. It won't take long before you realise it is the best thing you've ever done.'

The manufacturer did let the abusive client go, and after a hiatus this did indeed turn out to be the best move they had made. It wasn't easy, but they gradually won new business and stopped losing staff. Now the company is considerably better off than it was before, in terms of both in fee income and profit.

When I first started mentoring the company, this manufacturer's transition map showed it wanted to double its business over a three-year period. It would never have been able to achieve this unless it took the tough decision to change its pack. It takes a big intake of breath to do it but, believe me, it is always worth it in the end.

Whenever I find myself wavering, before taking a big step like this and ploughing on with my decision, I always draw inspiration from others who have done the same kind of thing. This could entail reading about inspirational people who have changed their circumstances and then succeeded against the odds. Alternatively, look up and look around you at people you know who should be daunted by their circumstances, fearing the worst possible outcome, yet press ahead anyway.

I did just this recently when I was training for the Clipper Round the World yacht race, which is one of my personal challenges that I will talk a little more about in chapter nine. On the occasion I am thinking of, it was only my second time on a boat and I was being battered around by gale-force winds. Aside from the fact I had the most appalling and debilitating seasickness, I was harbouring real doubts that the boat would stay upright. I was acutely aware that the majority of the people had as much – or, more accurately, as little – experience sailing as I did. Indeed, as I cast my eyes around the boat, I took in the sight of my fellow amateurs in a similar state of distress. Then, my gaze fell upon the skipper, who was standing at the helm. He had a cigarette in one hand and the wheel in the other, and was leaning back against the boat rail, looking for all the world like a man who had just ordered a pint in his favourite country pub. He was clearly utterly calm and clearly considered our situation to be completely normal.

I knew then that, to survive this training, I had to be part of his pack. While I didn't have the experience required to know I was safe, I could see the skipper did, and that was enough for me. I won't say the seasickness immediately vanished, because it didn't, but I certainly felt a great deal better after that.

Once you break free from your pack, you can replace its members with better role models, like this skipper. This is not to say you will immediately join the millionaire pack, if that is your aim, or that if you are a lower-league footballer you will walk into Premier League company. It may take several changes of pack as you progress towards your goal. If that is what it takes, so be it. The important thing is to keep moving steadily forward.

### Move on without regret

There is a fantastic American saying from the world of baseball: 'you can't steal second base with one foot on first'. It means, you can't move on with your life while you still have one foot in the past. You have to make that tough decision.

We are all guilty of hanging on to relationships for too long. Your pack may be made up of great people who you once really respected, yet maybe they have lost their way. They may not be too bothered about being success-ful, or even particularly happy, and might seem content to bump along doing nothing in particular. Even when life gets tough, they don't seem willing or able to change their situation.

There is a tendency to stand by people like this. Your long-held tie makes you feel somehow responsible for the people in your pack who can't or won't step up to the plate. You'll make excuses for them, saying things like, 'Doug had a really messy divorce four years ago and he's never recovered. I can't walk away now. What sort of person would that make me?'

Well, there are a number of ways of looking at this. While I would be the first to stand by a mate if he was in trouble, if he remains in trouble and refuses to help himself, I won't stand by him forever. It may sound callous, but there is only so much you can do before the situation will start pulling you down. As I always say, I will walk with those who want to walk and run with those who want to run, but I will never stand still for anyone. If I can see that someone is steadfastly refusing to help themselves, I do not hang around.

There is another way of looking at it too. If I make the tough decision and move on from my pack, there is the possibility I will be able to go back and help them once I have achieved my goals. Having followed my personal transition – changing my life by building and selling a multi-million-pound business – I am now giving something back to my community. My current transition involves an ambition to devote a third of my life to business, a third to my family and a third to charity work. Thus, on a volunteer basis, I devote much of my time to mentoring businesses and raising money for charitable groups. I use the knowledge I have gained over the years to coach people and help them out of their negative outlooks and into a more positive frame of mind.

In truth, there has been a time lag. I have not been able to help all the packs I have left behind over the years. To be brutally honest, though, could I ever have helped them properly while I was there anyway?

Look carefully at your transition map and ask yourself what you would be able to do for your previous packs once you had achieved your goals. You may be able to put something back into the community through charity work, or help others by leading by example. Sticking with the status quo doesn't help anyone. Make a decision about who is not right for your pack and change your outlook.

**Summary**
- Surround yourself with positive people who support and grow you towards your goals.
- Analyse the extent to which your key relationships help or hinder your achievements.
- Eliminate (or at least limit) contact with negative people.
- Remember to discount negative labels from negative people (see chapter two).

## ADDITIONAL PPA EXERCISE

Whether you decide to stick with your pack through thick and thin or walk away will vary considerably depend on your personality type. Some people are very receptive to the idea of having a clear-out of negative influences, while others will be tremendously loyal whatever the personal cost.

This section will give you some clues to understand how you are reacting to what you have read so far, in accordance with your personality type. It also gives some ideas on how you may best use this chapter for your own style of thinking and learning.

### Dominance messages
- You may think you can achieve your future state without the aid of other people, but you will achieve far more with their support, guidance and occasional prodding.
- When you objectively analyse the pluses and minuses of each key relationship, you will be surprised how much you benefit from some of them.
- Deal with negative people in a sensitive and respectful manner.

### Influence messages
- If the people around you do not support your ambitions, you need to find a new circle.
- Objectively analysing the pros and cons of each key relationship can be a painful process.
- It may be hard to cut yourself off from negative people, so focus on the dreams they are holding you back from realising.

### Steadiness messages
- Your loyalty to people can blind you to the fact that some do not support your ambitions.
- An objective analysis of each key relationship will identify those worth maintaining.
- Once you can see clearly that some people are dragging you down, you owe it to yourself to end that situation so that you can continue to work towards your future state.

### Compliance messages
- It is better to have a few good relationships than lots of unsatisfactory ones.
- Analysing the pros and cons of each key relationship will identify the positive people.
- Limit your exposure to negative people using logic and diplomacy.

CHAPTER NINE

# FIND YOUR EXCLAMATION MARK

Courage is not the absence of fear. It is the presence of fear, yet the will to

go on – Ambrose Hollingworth Redmoon

Without a doubt, one of the most challenging events of my life to date was walking along a 50-foot length of burning coals. Before and during this mind- and foot-numbing feat, I was fully aware that those coals were at a temperature of 1200°F (four times the maximum temperature of my oven at home) and could melt a slab of aluminium in a heartbeat. Just looking along the length before I set off made my heart pump with anticipation and I could feel rivers of adrenaline pounding through my body. I was acutely aware that logic dictated that this just wasn't possible, but I went ahead and did it anyway.

What you may well be thinking at this point is: why?

I walked on hot coals because I believe that we all have the capacity to turn our fears into power. Turning a belief like this into reality is nothing to do with learning some mystical technique, or finding a hidden paranormal skill within. I was able to embark on my journey because I restructured my mind. I was able to prove to myself that it is possible to overcome fears,

fbs@mikegreene.co.uk

limiting beliefs and phobias.

My fire walk was done under the tutelage of the inspirational motivational speaker Tony Robbins. It was the culmination of a four-day course in the lovely Hawaiian islands that covered everything to do with emotional, physical and financial mastery in the most uplifting way. Robbins argued very powerfully that, just because we become conditioned to believe something can't be done, it doesn't mean we are right. Nothing is impossible. If you believe in your own abilities, you can achieve anything.

And, as I discovered, self-belief is something you can't fake – particularly when you are expected to walk along hot coals to prove it!

I've often been asked since how it is possible to believe in something so strongly that you won't get burned by hot coals. One of the easiest ways to explain this is through the medium of auric (or Kirlian) photography. This is an advanced technique in which a camera is able to capture your aura. Your aura is basically the amount of energy you project and the intensity of your auric influence on physical things close to you. If you have a strong aura, it shows up as what you may think of as the 'Ready Brek glow', made famous by the TV ads of the seventies and eighties. In these adverts, children who ate this hot breakfast cereal all showed a dramatic, radiant glow that acted like a personal radiator to ward off the winter chill.

If people are feeling gloomy or under the weather, they will have virtually no auric glow. However, if they are really intense and bursting with energy, auric photography will pick up an energy field, which shows as light shooting out all around their bodies.

If you believe strongly that you can do something and are utterly convinced by your own power, your auric glow will appear like an amazing energy force field around you. You will be surrounded by a powerful light, invisible to the naked eye, yet powerful enough to protect you from virtually anything.

We all have the power to build up our self-belief and create that force field; once you do so, you will be able to walk over hot coals because you will be protected by the incredible force of your own self-belief.

If you've never seen a hot coal walk done, it is easy to be sceptical. People often try to rationalise how it is possible through scientific terms. They may even intimate that there is some sort of trickery involved. Everyone is, of course, entitled to their opinion, but let me add one further thought here. When I did my coal walk, I did it alongside a large group of around 1000 other people. Although it was most certainly a voyage of self-discovery, we all helped to build each other up and encouraged each other with chants and applause.

Out of that group of 1000, I witnessed around 60 people step off the path of hot coals because they had burned their feet (albeit not seriously, as they were able to step off as soon as any pain was felt). Being the curious sort, I asked a handful of them what had gone wrong. Each one gave me the same sort of answer.

'I was doing absolutely fine and then, suddenly, I lost concentration – I looked down and thought "What on earth am I doing?"' they said. 'That was the moment my skin started to burn.'

I am prepared to lay money on the fact that, if I had taken an auric photo of the unsuccessful coal-walkers in the few moments before they stepped off the path, they would have had the same healthy halo glow as the rest of us. Yet, if I had taken another one in the few seconds immediately before they leapt off, I strongly suspect it would have shown that their aura had shrunk rapidly as they became overwhelmed by doubts. Without that aura, or force field, to protect them, they didn't stand a chance of completing the walk.

None of this is to suggest that you heat up some coal and give this exercise a go. In fact, I would urge you most strongly not to do so. Fire-walking requires a degree of knowledge and training as well as faith in your own power. You need expert advice for that. No, what this chapter is about is challenging yourself to go further than you ever imagined you could. It is about developing your courage muscle so you are not afraid to take the big leaps you need to make in order to reach your ambitious goals.

You may never be able to truly eradicate your fears, but there are ways to get to understand them and know they are there, but get on with things anyway.

## Building your courage muscle

How often do you test yourself? I mean really test yourself? Not often enough, would be my guess. When things are going well, it is tempting not to do anything to rock the boat. After all, if you keep doing more of the same, what could possibly go wrong?

Everything.

If you don't constantly push yourself to the limits, you won't be growing as a person, you won't be challenging yourself and, well, you won't really be getting anywhere.

Think about it another way. If failure is the route to success, your goal should be to have a steady stream of challenges, some of which may end badly, in order to increase your chances of success. Indeed, if your goals on your transition map are as ambitious as they should be, you should be pushing yourself to the limits as often as you can.

Imagine, for example, a salesman. Say that, instead of setting himself a daily goal of having two prospects say 'yes', he declares that his day won't be over until he's been rejected, or heard the word 'no', ten times. Then imagine that the first two people he calls on say 'yes'. Rather than going home, happy to have filled his quota, he would be behind because he'd still need ten 'nos'. If he knew he didn't have to push himself hard, he wouldn't ever push or test himself to his limits. It is only by setting himself the toughest challenge there is that he would fulfil his true ability.

If he set himself a challenge like this, do you think his success rate would go up or down?

To overcome your fear of failure, you should be challenging yourself all the time, every day, and the key is to develop your courage muscle. Developing your courage muscle is just like developing any other muscle. You need to give it lots of exercise. Every time you challenge yourself, your courage muscle will get a little stronger. Step by challenging step, you will become a little better equipped to face any adversity that is thrown at you. Courage becomes a habit and, before long, you will wonder what you've been afraid of all this time.

You need to keep it up too because, just like every other muscle, your courage will fade if you don't regularly exercise it.

### The science bit

To get to the bottom of why we should all try to build our courage muscle, we need to talk a little bit about neurology and, most specifically, the principle neurons in the brain, called dendrites.

Think for a moment about the much-used analogy of the brain as a computer. Each of our more than 100 billion neurons has over 100,000 dendrites, which makes over 100 trillion constantly changing connections. These connections form into networks for basic functions (such as cleaning our teeth or doing up the buttons on a shirt) and also for more complex functions (such as reading, doing your job or driving a car). These networks are the reason we don't have to re-learn everything every time we attempt a task. They remember and do the work for us.

Think back to when you learned to drive a car. In the beginning you had to think hard about checking your mirrors and engaging the clutch before you crunched your way through the gears. You found out by trial and error how going too close to the curb generally ends up scrapping your wheel hubs. Attempting to think about all these things while trying not to crash into other road users was a nerve-wracking experience in your early days as a learner

---

**QUICK EXERCISE**

## Courage challenge

We've all done something courageous at one time or other. We've overcome our fears and tackled something we really didn't want to do. Looking back at times when you have risen to the challenge, what were your motivations at the time? If you find out, it may help to assuage doubts you have in the future.

Take some quiet time to think and write down some examples of things that you have done that were above and beyond. They may be things like:

• standing up to someone you've always feared
• speaking in public, despite your fear of talking to large groups
• going outside your comfort zone in a business situation.

Looking at your sheet of paper, can you see a pattern to your behaviour? Is there a common denominator, for example? Are you the sort of person who has to be pushed to your limits before you say enough is enough? Or do you take pride in standing up for the little guy?

Now you know what makes you overcome your fears, you can apply that motivation to other situations. If you find yourself telling yourself that you can't do something, think back to the time you did act out of character. Remind yourself of what spurred you on then, and stop telling yourself it can't be done. Don't hesitate – just do it.

As I said earlier, the more you practice courage, the easier it will feel. If you are the type of person who likes a bit of science to explain things, you may like the following section, which proves that this is an incontrovertible fact.

---

Now think about how you drive today. If you passed your test some time back, it is almost certain that, when you climb into your car, you won't give a second thought to a single one of those things that vexed you so much in the beginning. You'll just jump in and speed off from A to B, moving smoothly through the gears and keeping a safe distance from the curb. The reason you are able to do this is because those dendrites have created a super-highway in your brain.

Dendrites are created by repetitive behaviour. The first time you try something, it feels unfamiliar because there is no path for the dendrites to follow. Getting to your goal, or acquiring a new sort of behaviour, becomes like cutting a path through the jungle. The second time you try that path, it will feel a little easier, because many of the larger obstructions have already been moved. Each time you go down the path after that it will become easier and easier as the path gradually becomes trodden down and the way becomes clear. Eventually, after repeating the behaviour many times, you will have created that super-highway of dendrites and will be able to shoot along to your destination with barely a backwards glance.

Once a behaviour has become hard-wired into your neural network, the path will always be there. Unlike an elastic band, which snaps back into shape after being stretched, your network won't forget this acquired behaviour.

If you want to create new networks and learn to overcome your fears, all you need to do is direct your attention towards the matter in hand, and practice. With a little concentration, dedication and discipline it will only take a short time for the new behaviour to become second nature. Actions that would once have terrified you will seem so much easier and you may surprise yourself with how much more you will achieve when you are not held back by your fears.

I am living proof that this is possible. When someone says something can't be done, it is now hard-wired into me to make it happen and prove them wrong. It doesn't matter how daunting the task is, I will now set out to do it without a second thought. You can do this too.

Go on, start developing your courage muscle. In the next section I will show you how to take on even bigger challenges, to fast-track the creation of those courage dendrites.

### Finding your exclamation mark

One of my early mentors was a very clever man called Stuart Lawson. When I first started working with him he was CEO of a major retailer, and he is currently a senior partner at the consultancy KPMG, which specialises in turning around ailing firms to prepare for an eventual sale or corporate restructuring.

After we had spent a short time together, Stuart made the following observation: 'Mike, I know you are working hard and love what you do, but if you are not careful each year will blend into the other. You need to introduce some exclamation marks into the mix.'

I was a little at a loss as to what he meant and asked him to explain.

'You already challenge yourself on a daily basis and that is good,' he began. 'What you need to do now is once a year introduce what I call an exclamation mark into your life to punctuate each year. Go and climb a mountain, run a marathon, walk on hot coals. Do whatever it takes to stretch yourself to your limits and at the same time take you away completely from your day-to-day concerns. Something different from your "normal". It will change your outlook on everything.'

Like many people, my initial reaction was that I just didn't have the time to do that. I was working 24-7 building up my business and could barely find time to tuck my two daughters into bed as it was. I wasn't quite sure how the family would react if I told them I was off on a several-week-long 'exclamation mark', and I knew I wasn't that keen to leave them either.

Besides which, I argued, I always switch off at Christmas and when I am lounging by the pool on a hard-earned summer break with my family. Isn't that good enough?

Stuart's argument was that setting yourself extreme challenges is a way to detach yourself from the things that fill your mind every day. If, for example, your goals are all to do with business, the chances are you will be consumed by the details of running a company, finding new business and deciding whether or not it is the right time to expand. Alternatively, if your ambitions lie in turning your personal life around, your mind will be taken up with thoughts about diet, fitness, relationships and personal fulfilment. If your career features in your transition map, you will constantly be looking for the next opportunity for promotion, or ways to get yourself noticed.

If you are firmly focused on your goals, as indeed you should be, it is tough to step away.

Yes, we do all find some time during our rare breaks – such as weekends, family holidays or special occasions – to think about something else. But it is rare to be able to spend time totally removed from things and separated from 'normality'. We can't really complain about that – after all, it is perfectly fair and proper that family and close friends should make demands of us when we spend time with them. However, the result is that we are usually brought back to earth with a bump when the phone rings and you are called back to your day job (at any time of the day or night).

The truth is that a number of different elements are needed to make the rapid transition between where you are now and your goals for your future self. While it is essential for you to be focused intently on your goals – and, indeed, that is what much of this book is about – it will take more than just that to get you to your destination in the fast timescale you've set out. We have already talked about the need to regularly pause and take stock to make sure you are on track (see chapter seven). However, the final piece of the jigsaw, which will give you a 360-degree view of what you are doing (and the courage and rigour to get it done), is an annual challenge that will stretch you to your limits. This is what was referred to in the car analogy in chapter seven as the 'annual service', as opposed to the daily checks needed to keep things moving smoothly.

Your annual challenge, or exclamation mark, will draw you up, stop one year blending into the next and remind you to keep on your toes and keep challenging yourself all the time, every day. It should be the ultimate test for your courage muscle.

To properly fulfil the requirements of an exclamation mark, you need to completely detach yourself from all distractions. Ideally, the challenge you set yourself will be so different from your usual diversions that it will force you a long way from your comfort zone.

Your chosen activity should push you to your limits, because when we are at our most frustrated we learn something. You won't get very frustrated sitting by a pool sipping a piña colada, although this sort of relaxation has a place. No, to properly stretch yourself, you need to be somewhere where you reach the bottom of your emotional and physical strength. If you don't get to the point where you almost cry out loud ('Why am I doing this?') then you are not being pushed hard enough. But, when you do get to this point, and enter unchartered ground, you will discover remarkable things about yourself. This is the exclamation mark you need to reach and it will have a positive knock-on effect on how you spend your life for the rest of the year. By overcoming your big challenge, you will instantly create a courage super-highway through your dendrites in one go. After that, anything else you try to attempt in the year will seem like a walk in the park.

Ideally, you will undertake an exclamation mark at least once a year, to keep your courage muscle in peak fitness. This will support all the other ambitious plans you have for the rest of the year. I have undertaken at least one a year since Stuart suggested it and it has become an important part of my life.

One of my first challenges of this kind was to run a marathon. I am not a natural runner and don't particularly have a runner's build. However, I could see why I had to do it and set out to achieve it with vigour.

The training routine was a real trial for me. It was extremely physically demanding and took me to the edge of my emotions, too, because some days I really had to force myself to go out on the lengthy practice runs I needed to do. Yet it didn't take me long to see that those runs helped me to find something else within me. I soon came to value that hour or so I spent training for three or four days each week because it took me away from everything. It wasn't that I had one or two hours uninterrupted thought about my business. In fact, quite the opposite. I often didn't think of it at all. What it did was invigorate me and helped me build my courage muscle, which in turn helped me in every other aspect of my life and, of course, in the pursuit of my goals.

In each year's challenge, I try to push myself harder. Over the years I have run marathons, climbed Mt Meru and Mt Kilimanjaro, trekked 230 km around the Annapurna Circuit in Nepal (reaching 17,700 ft above sea level), cycled from London to Paris and climbed the highest mountains in Scotland, England and Wales (Ben Nevis, Scafell Pike and Snowden) within 24 hours. One of my most recent challenges has been to sign up for the Clipper Round the World yacht race. This one has particular emotional resonance for me because of an accident I had in my youth that has made me permanently wary of water.

It happened when was out fishing with my stepdad. I was only ten years old and had always loathed these trips. I just couldn't see the joy in sitting around a lake all day, staring into the water, waiting for something to happen. On the day in question, I had wandered off to stretch my legs and break the monotony. As I poked around the lake bank with a stick I'd selected from the many scattered around the ground, I spotted a fish that had become trapped in the roots of one of the trees that abutted the water's edge. The fish was clearly dead but, as it was the most interesting thing I had seen that day, I stooped down to take a closer look. Of course, the inevitable happened; I lost my footing on the slippery bank and plunged head first into the ice-cold water of the lake.

I was only in the lake for a few minutes before my stepdad waded in and fished me out with a firm and assertive grip on the collar of my sodden t-shirt. Even though the incident was over in a flash, I can still remember even now the feeling of fear, disorientation and icy wetness. It really shocked me and shook up my confidence. That memory has stuck with me all my life and is something I am always reminded of when I get near water. All of a sudden, I am my ten-year-old self all over again and I can recall how I felt after pitching into the lake. It is for this reason that I know a gruelling yacht race is something that will test me to my limits. After all, I will be deliberately putting myself in a position where I am 3000 miles away from the nearest source of rescue. However, although I know this will be a challenge, I welcome it. Experience has showed me it will be worth it.

When you choose your exclamation mark, try to avoid things that you are good at or comfortable with. Remember, this is supposed to be a challenge that takes you out of your comfort zone. If you are not a keen climber, tackle a mountain. If you've always hated running, sign up for a marathon. The more you detach yourself from things you feel comfortable with, the more you will build that courage muscle. And, when your courage muscle is stronger, why

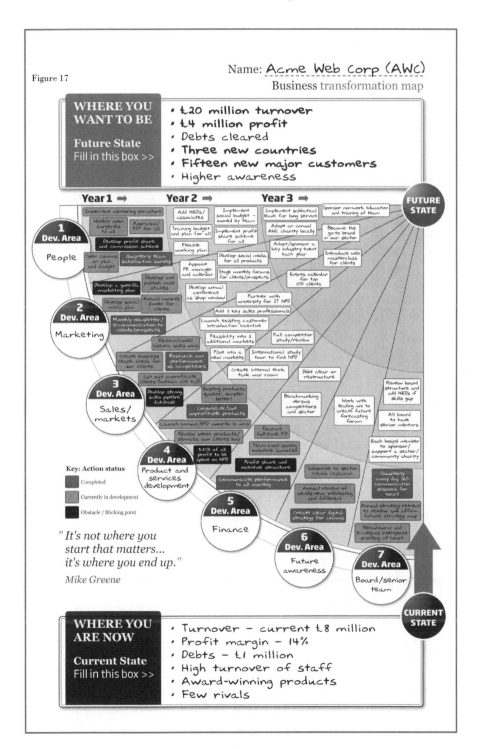

Figure 17

Name: Acme Web Corp (AWC)
Business transformation map

**WHERE YOU WANT TO BE**

**Future State**
Fill in this box >>

- £20 million turnover
- £4 million profit
- Debts cleared
- Three new countries
- Fifteen new major customers
- Higher awareness

"It's not where you start that matters... it's where you end up."
*Mike Greene*

**WHERE YOU ARE NOW**

**Current State**
Fill in this box >>

- Turnover – current £8 million
- Profit margin – 14%
- Debts – £1 million
- High turnover of staff
- Award-winning products
- Few rivals

not review your transition map once again, as we have done here with AWC in Figure 17?

---

### QUICK EXERCISE

## What would you do if you knew you couldn't fail?

Ask yourself the question above.

What risk would you take? What challenge would you try that you never imagined you would do? Is there something you dreamed of doing as a kid yet got discouraged from attempting by well-meaning adults?

Write it down.

Look at it.

Now, tell yourself: this is what people who are changing their lives do every day. So, why not try it?

Well, why not?

A strange thing happens when we really challenge ourselves. We start to realise that we are actually capable of much more than we had ever imagined. We realise that many of our long-held fears are groundless. In fact, by meeting and fulfilling our challenges, we realise that fear doesn't really exist until *we* say it does.

Once you've got this, think about your past failures. Did they mostly happen when you didn't try, or gave up trying? Well, now you know what can be done once you build up your courage muscle. So, feel the fear if you must. But do it anyway!

This would be a good time to revisit your transition map and add a few personal challenges. You should also take the opportunity to review whether your future state and goals are as stretched as they could be.... or were your first few attempts a little conservative? Why not up the ante a bit with your future state?

---

**Summary**
- With self-belief, anything is possible.
- The brain creates pathways for repeated behaviours, so practice taking risks.
- Set daily challenges to overcome a fear of failure.
- Set yourself an annual mega-challenge, or exclamation mark, that expands your 'normal'.

## ADDITIONAL PPA EXERCISE

The extent of your willingness to plunge yourself into challenging situations will depend on your personality type. Some people are very receptive to the idea of pushing themselves to their limits in unfamiliar situations, while others will always err on the side of caution. This will have a significant impact on how you tackle introducing exclamation marks into your life.

This section will give you some clues to understand how you are reacting to what you have read so far, in accordance with your personality type. It also gives some ideas on how you may best use this chapter for your own style of thinking and learning.

### Dominance messages
- Believe in your single-mindedness to achieve your goals.
- Practice taking risks until it becomes normal to do so.
- Challenge yourself each day to go ever further.
- Embrace an annual 'exclamation mark'.

### Influence messages
- Believe in your passion to be a success.
- Practice taking risks until it becomes an enjoyable habit.
- Challenge yourself each day to greater heights.
- Embrace an annual 'exclamation mark'.

### Steadiness messages
- Believe in your determination to deliver what you set out to do.
- Practice taking risks until it becomes routine.
- Challenge yourself each day to go outside your comfort zone.
- Embrace an annual 'exclamation mark'.

### Compliance messages
- Believe in your pursuit of excellence.
- Practice taking risks until it becomes a regular habit.
- Challenge yourself daily to push your boundaries.
- Embrace an annual 'exclamation mark'.

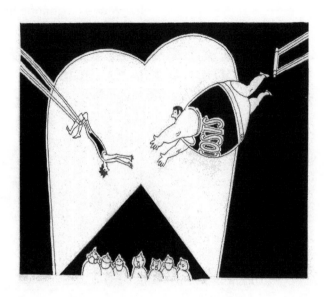

**CHAPTER TEN**

# SUCCESS IS NOT A LINEAR PATH

*The quality of your life is in direct proportion to the amount of uncertainty*

*you can comfortably live with – Tony Robbins*

It was one of those awful moments. A decision made in a split second with barely a second thought and one that ended up costing half a million pounds. When it comes to failures, I am quite well qualified to talk about them because I once cost my employer an extraordinary amount of cash.

Let me begin at the beginning. It happened fairly early on in my career, not long after I had managed to turn my life around following my bankruptcy. I had a job with the oil giant Conoco (today known as Conoco Philips) running its managed shops department. This meant I worked with the retail side of its petrol forecourts, negotiating terms with buying groups, organising promotions and developing new sites. I was also responsible for determining the shop sales potential of new sites, which strongly affected how much we would be prepared to pay for the sites. Competition was always fierce because we didn't want to lose out to our rivals (BP, Shell and Esso).

By all accounts I had carved out a good niche for myself and had proved to be pretty good at my job in the three years since I had joined Conoco.

In my first year I had increased profits in the department by 38 per cent, then 27 per cent in the following year and 32 per cent the year after that. I enjoyed the work and felt confident that I knew the ropes and could spot any problems a mile off. Clearly, as it turned out, I was completely wrong about that.

It all began innocuously enough. Conoco was in negotiations to buy 11 privately held petrol stations from their two joint owners and I had a meeting booked in with the two men in question to discuss the retail side of things. A week earlier, when the meeting had first been arranged, I had requested a report about the 11 sites from Conoco's demographic profiling analysts. This report would set out information about the customer base in the area of the forecourts in question – social status, income and so on. I'd had dozens of these reports written for me in the past for various sites because they are a useful tool to work out ways to boost the customer's experience and therefore the company's profits.

For some reason, the demographic profiling department was a little slower than usual compiling this report and I didn't receive it until the morning of the meeting with the two garage owners. Still, although I was a little cross about the delay, I barely gave the report a second glance as I dashed off to the rendezvous. If I thought about it at all, I was just confident that I had seen enough of these documents to be pretty sure of the contents.

The meeting seemed to go well and the sellers appeared to be warming to Conoco's offer of £2.5 million for a handful of the sites. They said they still needed more time to chew it over between them and as a parting shot I handed over the demographic profiling report, urging them to come back to me if they had any further questions.

The following morning, which was a Friday, I got a call from the chief executive's office.

'Mike, could you please come in to see Barry first thing Monday?' said the secretary, who seemed to be steadfastly avoiding explaining what the meeting was about.

Even so, I instantly knew it was not going to be good news. I understood enough of the corporate world to instinctively know that a slap on the back and congratulations always happen straight away. Bad news tends to be left to simmer for a few days before it's served up.

As you can imagine, I had a pretty miserable weekend wondering what on earth I had done. By the time I arrived at Barry Quinn's office on Monday morning, I was already fearing the worst. But the news, when it came, was far more devastating than I could ever have imagined.

It turned out that, in their wisdom, the demographic profiling department had decided to introduce a new formula to their reports. Unbeknownst to me, in the updated style they now recorded Conoco's valuation of the asset in question in the document itself.

There it was in black and white: Conoco's declaration that they believed these forecourts were worth £3 million.

And they'd only offered £2.5 million.

Clearly, there was no longer much room for negotiation now I had blithely handed the two sellers a document stating the higher price.

I could hardly believe my mistake. Why the hell hadn't I stopped for a moment and checked the report? What a stupid, stupid thing to do. For a moment I felt physically sick with the realisation I had just lost the company £500,000, if not the sale altogether. That sort of careless mistake would be more than enough to see an executive summarily dismissed from most companies.

Barry had a very interesting way of dealing with my failure, though, and went on to give me a lesson that I have drawn upon throughout my life ever since.

'I know you well enough Mike to know that what you did was not done with ill intent,' he told me, as I sat in front of him still numb with shock. 'Plus, it is such a stupid mistake, I'm convinced you could not have even been aware that you made it.

'Luckily for you, you have made an exceptional amount of money for the company over the years you have been with us, otherwise we may have been having a very different conversation today.'

What Barry was saying was, yes, I had screwed up massively, but he was content to look at the bigger picture and what I had achieved for the company over the past three years. By acknowledging my successes, as well as my massive failure, he made a huge deposit in my emotional bank account. In effect, by giving me another chance, he ensured my complete and unerring loyalty to the company. In addition, of course, he knew as well as I did that I would never make the same mistake again.

Although it hurt – and even today I still remember the acute feeling of shame, embarrassment and regret – I learned so much from this failure. It is not great to make mistakes, but they do happen occasionally. What is important is that you know how to deal with them, are prepared to work hard to get through them and, most of all, that you do not allow yourself to be hampered by a fear of screwing up in the future.

Fearing what may happen next if we do this or that holds us back all too often. We agonise over thoughts such as, 'What could go wrong if I make this decision? What will failing mean to me?'

I would argue that, as this experience shows, failure can be painful, but it is rarely fatal. If you have done enough hard work already, you will have a strong foundation to protect you from the fallout of getting something wrong. I will talk more about that strong foundation later in this chapter.

Most importantly: failure usually turns out to be a good thing because a big failure means you are pushing yourself to your limits.

## The road to success is not straight and never all upwards

The traditional view of success generally goes something like Figure 18:

- start
- go to a good school
- get a good job or start a business
- work hard
- get promoted or expand the business
- reach the top of your profession
- finish – be prosperous and happy.

*Figure 18*

In reality, success is nothing like this. If you have got this far in this book, you are hopefully well on the way to achieving whatever is your notion of success. Now it is time for the health warning.

Success is not a linear path.

If you expect it to be, you are in for a big disappointment.

Success rarely, if ever, goes in a straight line from bottom to top for anyone. Indeed, if you read the biography of any notable person, you will see their route to the top was littered with disappointment and failures.

I like to compare the path to success to a mountain climb. As a person who has climbed a number of mountains, including Kilimanjaro, I can attest to the fact that it is simply not possible to start at the bottom and ascend steadily to the summit in a nice straight line. Mountains are not that obliging. No, as Figure 19 shows, in order to reach the top you frequently have to descend to a lower altitude in order to follow the natural rise and fall of the mountain. This uneven path occurs on virtually every journey, real or hypothetical, however ultimately successful the traveller turns out to be. In

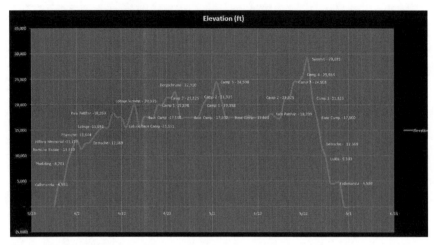

*Figure 19*

a corporate setting, for example, if you looked closely at a company such as the hugely successful IT giant Apple, you'd be amazed at how the share price zigzags up and down over time. In a typical day it can gain or lose 10 or 20 cents, and over a year $3 or more. The important thing is, as you can see from Figure 20, which shows Apple's share price graph for 2012, the overall trend is upwards.

Even companies such as Apple, which are held up as the success stories

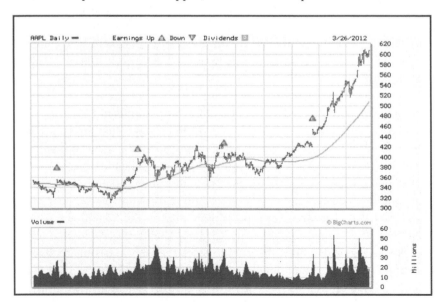

*Figure 20*

of their generation, will grow and consolidate, surge forward and then reign back. It is part of the natural ebb and flow.

---

## QUICK EXERCISE

### Check out your visions of success – success is not always what you think

To really understand the reality that not all success is uphill, try these two quick exercises.

1. Choose the company that you most admire and search the internet for its share-price graph (i.e. type 'Tesco share price graph' or 'Google share price graph' or 'Masterfoods share price graph' – you get the picture). It doesn't matter which company you pick – I guarantee that you will see a chart that looks like a mountain range of peaks and troughs, despite the fact that people on the outside of a company often perceive its overall growth as having been easy. It's the peaks' mid-to-long-term trend that is important and that counts, not the hourly or weekly troughs.

2. Think of and write down a sport, game, skill or subject that you are very good at, or above average. Think back to when you first started. How much did you know? How competent or confident were you when you first experienced the sport, game, skill or subject? Was your improvement all positive, or did you make the odd failure, mistake or slip in performance? What made you keep it up and why didn't you quit? Understanding some of these drivers can help you replicate this success in other areas.

You will find on this journey that, the further you climb your own 'mountain' towards your goal, the harder it will seem. It may even appear like you are constantly taking several steps back in order to make the big advances. That's fine. There is no need to panic. The final bit is always the hardest. After all, if it were easy, everyone would do it.

If you begin to find yourself dragged down by concerns that you seem to be taking a lot more reverse steps than forward ones, pause for a moment and take a good look at the bigger picture. Ask yourself whether you have had a successful day, or week, or even year. If

---

you're truly honest, have you been following your transition map faithfully? If the answer is that you have been working very hard indeed and that, overall, you are definitely following an upward trend, stop beating yourself up. Once you've recognised that there are going to be ups and downs, and that you will experience failures, you will be able to climb higher than you ever believed you could.

The biggest danger of all is that, as things begin to get tough, you will give up or turn back because the cost of failure seems too high.

## Climb high, sleep low

If you can accept that failure is a necessary part of the journey towards success, the good news is that it is possible to at least partly mitigate slip-ups and prepare yourself better for some knocks along the way.

To explain how this might work, I'd like to stick with the mountaineering analogy. There is a technique that I learned from my mountaineering experiences that perfectly parallels this case. The technique is known as 'climb high, sleep low'. Basically, it is a way of fooling your body into being able to climb far greater heights than it might otherwise be able to do. Indeed, you can push your body to ascend more than 1000 extra feet a day by using this method.

How does it work? Well, the body does not usually react well to climbing to a high altitude, for a number of reasons, one of which is that the amount of oxygen in the air is reduced and therefore it is harder to breathe. The body needs time to adjust to changes in height and, if climbers attempt to go up a mountain too quickly, they put themselves at risk of altitude sickness, which is a very dangerous and life-threatening condition. If a climber starts to show signs of altitude sickness, the accepted advice is to immediately descend a few hundred metres, whereupon the climber should make a full recovery.

Having carefully examined this phenomenon, climbing experts have worked out that it is possible to trick the body into believing it is at a higher altitude in order to be able to climb further quicker. When ascending a large mountain, the accepted technique is to always climb a few hundred metres further than you intend to go each day and then drop back that distance before making camp for the night. While you sleep at a lower altitude, your body will create more red blood cells and pump more oxygen around because it will believe it is still at a higher altitude. Thus, the climb the following morning is much easier and climbers are able to cover a far greater distance without causing discomfort or risk.

You can transfer this theory to all sorts of other situations. Climb high, sleep low is about accepting that your journey won't be easy but going for it anyway, having utilised as many things as possible that are in your favour and having sought help from all available sources.

Thus, for example, you may like to look at examples of others who have trodden your path. You may be able to climb higher by looking at how they achieved their goals. What lessons can you learn from the way they did so? How could they help to ease your passage towards your own target?

It is also important to be aware of times when you *shouldn't* be motoring ahead full-speed towards your target. Take a business setting, for example. In your fast track to success, let's say that there are signs of problems – perhaps staff are resistant, or there are technical difficulties that mean it is not easy for you to keep up with the pace of change. If this is the case, you can ease up a little bit (descend) and take the time to put right whatever it is that needs addressing. Then, as soon as the blockage is sorted out, you can rapidly get back on your way and proceed at the same fast pace as before.

Don't, however, allow the slower pace to become your norm. Once you become comfortable at a reduced rate of action, it can be very difficult to pick up the pace. It becomes the accepted speed. Instead, accept that you wish to continue as before but are easing the altitude for one 'night' (the briefest period possible) in order to continue your relentless assent to the top.

There are far too many large companies that put up with second best, or get stuck in the rut of a slower pace. Directors will talk to investors and the press about their vision to grow 1 or 2 per cent, making out that it is a challenging goal. They don't want to promise anything ambitious like 15 per cent growth in case they fail and find themselves on the receiving end of brickbats and lose out on their bonuses. The reality is that, once these companies have set these soft goals, everyone works towards the sluggish low-single-digit growth – no more, no less. The workforce may be perfectly capable of reaching 15 or even 20 per cent if encouraged, but, if no one ever pushes them, they will never realise their potential. What a waste. Those directors have set up an environment of non-achievement.

### Build a firm foundation

Climb high, sleep low is not the only way to mitigate the potential fallout from failure. Another great technique is to lessen the chances of things going wrong in the first place, or at the very least acquire enough experience and knowledge to rise above any problems that might occur. Doing this takes a strong foundation, and this is something you should seek to build at the earliest opportunity.

To explain how this might work, let's return once again to the perceived notions regarding an 'ideal' life. The example in Figure 21 shows a 'perfect' career in retailing, in which a youngster starts off as a shop assistant in a retail company and rises through the ranks to become a store manager, then an area manager, and on and on, up to eventually taking over as the chief executive. You can of course adapt this to your own circumstances and whether your focus is on running a business, managing a career or sorting out your personal life. The boxes will be filled in differently, but the principles will be the same. Most people have aspirations to move in an unrelenting straight line towards the goal at the top.

You don't have to be a structural engineer to realise that the foundations of the construction in Figure 21 are pretty shaky. In fact, they are more shaky than the Leaning Tower of Pisa! It is hard to see how the whole thing is still standing, and if I were to reach the CEO position in this scenario I would be feeling very vulnerable indeed.

Yet, this is the progression most people imagine.

With a structure like this, it is little wonder that sometimes things come a cropper or don't quite work as smoothly as planned. A little problem could prove a massive disaster and send the whole construction crashing to the ground.

To me it is obvious that, if you wish to avoid the pitfalls presented by this shaky structure, you need to put a solid foundation in place.

How might this work? Well, to continue the example in Figure 21, let's imagine we are mentoring the youngster in the first-jobber position. This person is keen to get on the ladder and step up to the sales-assistant role and from there up through the ranks. He may be frustrated by the fact that the person who

*Figure 21*

is currently in the sales-assistant job doesn't seem ready to relinquish the role; promotional opportunities may seem slow in coming.

What this first jobber should be asking themselves is this: what does the person above me have that I don't have? The obvious answer is experience. Ah, the first jobber may say, but how can I get experience if I don't get the promotion? My reply to this would be: why not take a side step for a while to get that experience? Go on a course, ask whether you can shadow someone who is in a more senior role or request a transfer to another department completely.

If the first jobber did this, their skills pyramid might look something like Figure 22.

A side step may only last a month, or perhaps a year, but it will transform this first jobber's understanding of what is ahead. Suddenly, the next stage in the plan will have a really solid foundation. That first jobber will know the 'language' spoken in the next stage, and have an idea of what to expect and how to excel. He will also be confident in his abilities and able to cope when things don't go as planned. Not all steps need to be upward.

If you did this at every stage, imagine how strong your foundation would be once you'd reached the top. You'd be virtually indestructible! I know for sure that my broad experience – in everything from shelf stacking to being a paper boy to working on the road in store development – all added up to a strong substructure that was vital when I came to run my own retail group. Time taken to learn and prepare yourself for the next day's challenge is never time wasted.

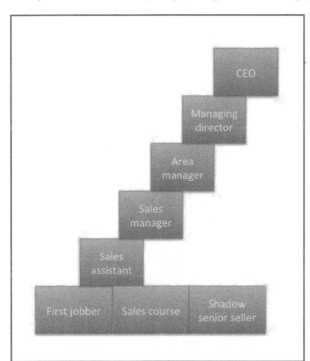

*Figure 22*

---

### QUICK EXERCISE

## Check your foundations

Draw up a pyramid for your own career or personal development to establish how firm the foundation of your success is. Either do this for your current state or imagine your future state and chart your proposed development. This exercise will show you in an instant the areas where you need to acquire skills to build the best possible foundation for the future.

Don't ever be afraid to take a side step. People often deride side steps as a negative thing. But, knowing what you know now, you should realise that they build a truly solid structure that will protect you when things don't go to plan. That is what matters, not what other people say.

We all face circumstances that cause us to alter our plans every day. If you want to make any progress, you have to be prepared and equipped with as much knowledge as possible. If, added to this, you are flexible and accept that your path to your destination will not be smooth, you will be able to get through pretty much anything.

---

### You can't completely avoid failure – nor should you try to

Failure is not a disaster. In fact, it is an important part of the process of trying to achieve something big. Think about it this way: if you get something right the first time, even every time, how creative are you going to be in your thinking as time goes on? Your goals, and attaining them, will almost become routine. Your brain won't be attuned to solving problems that have not been solved before because, well, it has never had to.

While you can mitigate the effects of failure and make sure you are strong enough to cope, don't ever get into a situation where you are completely averse to screwing up. Indeed, why not go one step further and actively welcome the odd mistake?

I read once that Sir James Dyson, the British inventor and founder of Dyson, said that you shouldn't just embrace failure; you should get a kick out of it.[9] Seeing as this comes from a person who went through 5126 prototype versions of his now famous dual-cyclone vacuum before he got it right, you

---

9. Nadia Goodman, 'James Dyson on using failure to drive success'. *Entrepreneur*, 5 November 2012. www.entrepreneur.com/blog/224855.

have to concede he may have a point. Sir James enjoyed the act of problem-solving and, as any ambitious plan holds a mountain of problems to solve, that is not a bad attitude to have. It is certainly a lot more constructive than scuttling for the exit every time there is a small setback.

This is not to say you should sit down and scrutinise every hiccup along the way. It is often said that you should *learn* from failure; the implication is that, if you pick apart your situation, you will somehow acquire a miracle formula that will ensure you never have a problem again.

That theory is OK, as far as it goes, but look at it another way. If you spend your life with your face turned backwards, sooner or later you are going to trip over a new hazard that you won't have seen right there in front of you.

Similarly, if you are too intent on learning that all-important lesson, you will become risk averse. The reality is that anything you do at speed, this transition included, will hold some risk. If you ran up the stairs at full pelt every day, sooner or later you will trip up. Now, you could slow down to a steady walk, but that means each day it will take you twice as long to get to your destination. You won't achieve anything extraordinary with an attitude like that.

You will screw up and fall over now and again. Get used to it.

Don't fall into the trap of being so blinded by your ambitions that you are unduly hard on anyone who doesn't always come up to scratch, either. If you are running a business or working with others towards your transition goals, you should encourage them to view failure in the same way as you do. It's going to happen, so expect it and get over it. Encourage this adventurous and free-thinking attitude in those around you. Create an atmosphere where mistakes are not criticised and people are helped to embrace a culture that is curious, determined and open to trial and failure.

You and the people around you have got to be free to try things out. That means avoiding the 'blame game' that infects so many businesses.

I had a great lesson in how this might work in practice from another Conoco executive, in a separate incident to the half-a-million-pound error described at the beginning of this chapter. It was another excellent example of leadership from within the oil company.

Ten months into the financial year, I found myself in a situation where I faced a massive overspend on my marketing budget. Instead of still having £100,000 left, as I had imagined, I discovered that my department had actually already spent £60,000 *over* the annual budget.

The mistake was down to an accounting error that was discovered very late in the day. There was no way I could go to the board and lay the blame on my finance team. There is a very strict hierarchy in business and I would have, quite rightly, got short shrift for pointing the finger at those below me. As the leader of the team, I was very much accountable for any screw-ups.

The fact that it was the right thing to do didn't make it any easier when I went to break the news to my immediate boss, marketing director Mike Stannard, another great leader who had obviously developed in the same Conoco culture as Barry Quinn. Worse still, I knew I had to tell him not only that my department had massively over-spent but also that we still owed money to contractors for marketing projects.

'That is a problem, isn't it?' he said, giving away no trace of emotion after I had laid out my position.

Then, with a smile that indicated that the meeting was coming to a close, he said: 'I'm sure you'll find a way around it. In fact, why don't you go to the other department heads and ask if you can have a little slice of their budget?'

Mike knew as well as I did that to go to my peers, admit to them I had screwed up and then ask for some of their budget was just about the toughest ask there could be. There would be the pain of having to endure their suppressed laughter at my humiliation and the added proviso that in the future I would be utterly beholden to them. If they needed a favour, I would be in pole position, whether it worked out for me or not.

Mike's solution really did make me squirm but I followed his advice and sang for my supper. My colleagues came up trumps and I managed to get myself out of the hole.

Once the initial fuss had died down, I reflected more deeply upon what had just happened. Conoco was a huge company with a multi-million-pound turnover. An overspend of £60,000 was a drop in the ocean; an accountant could cough and lose that much on the balance sheet. Mike Stannard could have easily said to me, 'Hey Mike, these things happen; don't do it again,' and then added a further £100,000 to my budget to see me through. Instead, he made me pay the price of my department's mistake and experience what it took to get out of it. It was rather like a parent letting a child fall off their bike. I found a way to look at things differently. Yes, it was tough, but it was a lesson that stuck. It was something I would always remember and would do all that I could to avoid going through again.

However, I didn't specifically *learn* from my mistake; what I did was become a better person by working out how to solve it. It became part of my 'experience bank' and something that, while I wouldn't want to repeat it, made me aware of what I shouldn't do in the future.

Don't focus too much on 'learning from mistakes'. The danger is that you will always go where you focus, because, as we saw earlier, if you focus on something else (as Amelia did with the bird in chapter four), you may well find yourself heading towards a ditch. Instead, concentrate your energies on your goal and what you need to get you there.

There are multiple paths to every destination, but don't ever allow yourself to be knocked off track if your best-laid plans go awry. That way, like a taxi driver who finds side streets and alternative routes around a jam, your brain will learn to be quick-minded in finding another route once you have been through 'the knowledge' of developing your ability to see failure for what it is: experience. Failures are simply part of your experience bank along the way. Plus, you will enjoy success so much more, knowing how tough it was to get there.

Remember, there are no such things as problems: there are only opportunities and challenges. Remain positive and focused and prepared to take the odd side step, and you will always reach the top of your mountain.

**Summary**
- Success is not linear so prepare for ups and downs, and side steps.
- Build a strong foundation.
- Encourage experimentation and avoid blame.
- Focus on forward-looking problem-solving and avoid backwards-looking postmortems.

## ADDITIONAL PPA EXERCISE

Your attitude to dealing with failure will depend substantially on your personality type. Some people are very quick to get over knock backs, while others will take things very personally. How will failures affect you and what should you do to stay on the right track?

This section will give you some clues to understand how you are reacting to what you have read so far, in accordance with your personality type. It also gives some ideas on how you may best use this chapter for your own style of thinking and learning.

### Dominance messages
- See ups and downs as challenges.
- Build a robust foundation for your transition.
- Encourage experimentation and tolerate the failures that may

come with that.
- Don't look back to allocate blame, just solve problems for the future.

**Influence messages**
- Anticipate ups and downs and enjoy the ride.
- Build a resilient foundation for your transition.
- Encourage creativity and accept the associated occasional misjudgements.
- Focus on doing things better in future.

**Steadiness messages**
- Be prepared to respond flexibly and quickly to unplanned events.
- Build a stable foundation for your transition.
- Encourage innovation as the route to growth.
- Don't repeat the mistakes of the past; instead design a better future.

**Compliance messages**
- Expect the unexpected and adjust your plans speedily.
- Build a solid foundation for your transition.
- Encourage trial and error in pursuit of continuous improvement.
- Don't waste time on lengthy postmortems when things go wrong; pick out the key learning points and drive forward with new insights.

## AFTERWORD

*A ship will rot out faster sitting in the harbour than if on the high seas, a plane will rust out quicker sitting on the tarmac than it will being flown everyday, a vacant home will certainly deteriorate quickly if someone isn't living in it and taking care of it. – Zig Ziglar*

In *Failure Breeds Success,* we have explored how to work out our own version of success, set firm goals and find ways to achieve them. We've looked at the labels we may have been erroneously given and the packs we surround ourselves with despite the fact that their members may often hold us back. We've set out strategies to free ourselves from negative influences and take control of our destinies. We've even talked about climbing a mountain or two, both literally and metaphorically. To keep things simple and on track, there has been a central theme of a transition map, which is an essential guide on your journey to the successful you. To help you in this quest, I've shown you how to break down your goals into achievable, bite-sized activities.

Now, in the closing pages of this book, it is time to add a *big* health warning.

None of this means a jot until you actually get on with it and do it! You can have the most impressive, detailed, full-colour, all singing, all dancing transition map ever, bursting with the most extraordinary ideas and goals, but, until you actually get on with it and take the first steps, that map is just a piece of paper.

As I outlined at the start of the book, this type of scenario happens all the time in the business world. Someone in management will make a big hoo-ha about producing a business plan. It will be discussed endlessly at management meetings, and revised, updated and polished. Eventually everyone will declare themselves satisfied and it will be presented breathlessly to anyone on the team who has not yet been fortunate enough to have seen it. Lofty goals will be flagged up, big numbers will be discussed and everyone will appear to be very excited.

Three months later, not one thing will have changed and the firm in question will be no nearer to achieving, or even setting out upon, these ambitions. Why? After all, the plan was refined to within an inch of its life. Well, most probably this is because the plan was tucked up on a shelf and forgotten about in the aftermath of the euphoria of having completed it.

The problem is, whether you are an individual or a company, if you remain where you are and do the same thing as you always have, you will stay where you have always been. Your goals will remain a distant dream and pretty soon you will probably end up throwing away your business plan or transition map because it is a rather unpleasant physical reminder that you failed to do anything.

Do you know what is even worse? If you continue to do nothing, you will more than likely actually end up in a *poorer* position than where you first started. It is an unfortunate law of nature that, while our bodies and minds would often rather stay at rest, if they are not regularly exercised and stretched they will actually deteriorate. The opening quote of this chapter, from inspirational motivational speaker Zig Ziglar, captures this phenomenon perfectly. Using the analogy of a ship that will rot if simply left in its harbour, or a plane that will rust if left on the tarmac, he illustrates how damaging it can be to stick with the status quo.

We were not made to be static and do nothing. Our bodies and minds need to be constantly challenged and stretched to their limits! Indeed, as countless scientific studies have shown, the more we stretch our muscles (and our brains), the stronger they get. Work hard and everything will be enhanced to help you do the job.

Don't be afraid that your body or brain will let you down. They won't. As countless other people have proved throughout history, there are no limits to what the human body and mind can achieve given half the chance. People who have repeatedly stretched themselves just that bit further have gone on to achieve the most incredible feats. There is absolutely no reason why this shouldn't be you. In fact, if it isn't you are wasting your potential.

What you decide to do now is up to you, though. You and only you can make the decision to go on this journey. You also have to do it in the knowledge that, even if you do take the brave decision and get started, there are no guarantees that you will attain all, or indeed any, of your three-year goals successfully. Although many people reading this book will hopefully be inspired enough to begin the journey I have outlined here, not everyone will complete it. People will lose heart when they encounter setbacks, get distracted by other things going on in their lives, or simply lose their way. Indeed, if you have been as ambitious as you should be in setting your targets, very few of you will make it all the way to a successful conclusion. But no one said transforming your life would be easy, and hopefully the tips I have outlined on dealing with – even welcoming – failure will help you overcome the setbacks.

The most important thing is that you try and give it your all. As I say here, we all have the capacity to succeed. We just need to be determined and do the right thing.

There are many things you can do to make sure you are one of the ones who makes it. If you follow the advice in this book and get into the *habit* of doing so as quickly and consistently as possible, that will be a great start. The reason so many New Year's resolutions fail is that people slip back into their old routine almost immediately. They don't deliberately make time to exercise, or start a new hobby, or whatever they have vowed to do. With no time set aside, it is hardly surprising that they fail at the start line. If you want to change your life, you need to make your new existence a habit.

It is also essential to make sure that your transition map is a *physical* document. I have had people tell me in the past that their map was 'in their head' and they knew exactly where they were heading. 'No you don't,' I say. 'You are wasting your time. You have to write down your goals.'

The discipline of writing something down is the first step in making it happen. If it is there in black and white, you won't be able to fool yourself at a later date that you 'never really meant that you wanted to go that far'.

Once you have done a transition map, make it the focus of your life and put a printout of it somewhere where it will constantly interrupt you. Better still, stick one up in several locations so you can't miss it! Don't let it be like the business plan I mentioned earlier, which gets left to moulder on a shelf. You could stick copies to your car visor, your fridge door, the inside of your wardrobe door or food cupboard, your bathroom mirror – anywhere you might spot it on a day-to-day basis. Leave it anywhere where it will interrupt your day and remind you of what you are setting out to achieve.

If at any time it starts to feel a bit tough, or things don't go quite as planned, go back to the map. Remind yourself why you are doing this and remember the amazing goals that you have set out to achieve. Take a look at some of the motivating pictures you have added to your map and imagine how you will feel when you reward yourself with that holiday, or that expensive watch, or whatever bonus it is that you have inserted to help you along the way.

If you don't feel that you are making progress, use some of the meditative techniques outlined in this book to pause for a moment and think about what you have done more deeply. The chances are that, when you do, you will find that you've gone far further than you ever imagined possible. You'll probably even surprise yourself.

Don't be shy about sharing your achievements, either. There is nothing like vocalising what you have achieved to really crystallise in your mind just how far you have come. I'd love you to share your progress with me, too, and you can do so via my website: www.mikegreene.co.uk/fbs. There is a great forum on there where you can share some of your successes and challenges with others who are going through the same process. Who knows, you may even be able to inspire others to achieve greater things, too, and there can be no better feeling than that.

Your personal development does not need to end here, though. Two of the overriding themes in this book are turning setbacks into triumphs and learning how to overcome challenges that send ordinary folk into a tailspin. As the title of the book promises, there is always a way to turn failures into successes, make negatives positive and not be utterly crushed by every setback.

There is, however, an opportunity to take this one stage further. Imagine what you could achieve if you didn't just 'cope' with setbacks, or find a way to transform them into positives, but you actually *actively encouraged them*. Yes, I am talking about *trying to fail*.

It is my contention that, if you wish to achieve true and outstanding success, you have to seek out failure. This is the focus of my second book, *Head for the Eye of the Storm – A Fast Track to Success*. My inspiration came from my latest exclamation mark, in which I signed up for a few legs of the Clipper Round the World yacht race. It is an event that gives amateur sailors the chance to test their mettle by crewing a boat in a highly challenging race. I have had virtually no experience as a sailor and, as I detailed earlier in this book, have not always had the best relationship with water, so, when I joined the initial briefing for the race, I hung on to the instructor's every word.

One of the first things I was told stopped me in my tracks: 'We'll do a day or two of classroom training before we plug in the GPS and find a storm or two we can get to in the shortest time,' smiled one of the boat skippers. 'Then, we'll head into the eye of the storm.'

Just as I was mulling over the full implications of this in my mind and considering how I might fare alongside a crew of complete amateurs in one of the most dangerous situations on earth (or, more precisely, sea), one of my fellow sailors piped up to voice what we were all privately thinking.

'But, we're all amateurs,' he said. 'How will we know how to cope?'

The skipper was clearly used to answering this question, but still managed to deliver his view with enthusiasm and encouragement.

'We can teach you lots in the classroom or moorings, but there is no way we can prepare you for this kind of experience on calm seas, and certainly not in the confines of a classroom,' he said. 'We have to take you out into a storm or you will never be as successful as you need to be.'

He was, of course, entirely right. Understanding, and indeed welcoming, the potential to fail is an important part of this journey, and indeed any journey. Realising this prompted me to write a follow-up to *Failure Breeds Success*. While *Failure Breeds Success* is a lesson in setting ambitious goals while accepting, embracing and learning from life's ups and downs, *Head for the Eye of the Storm* goes one step further. It explores the opportunities that are presented to you when you don't just accept and deal with failure, but when you actively seek it out.

We can all tick along, getting things right sometimes and then correcting them when they go awry, but it is only when you head straight for the eye of the storm that you really find out what you are capable of.

When you deliberately seek out a challenge like this, it will be the toughest journey you will ever make, but the rewards will far outweigh the hardship. A willingness to fail, or even an active attempt to push the boundaries where there is very little chance of success, is the only way to make the big breakthroughs.

Having read *Failure Breeds Success*, you are already on the road to your ultimate goals. Are you now ready to take the fast track to success?

*Head for the Eye of the Storm*, by Mike Greene, will be published in January 2014.

For advance copies go to www.mikegreene.co.uk/eofts.